W9-CRU-869

THE INCOMPARABLE CHRIST

BILLY E. SIMMONS

BROADMAN PRESS
Nashville, Tennessee

© Copyright 1980 • Broadman Press.
All rights reserved.
4251-71
ISBN: 0-8054-5171-4

Scripture passages marked NASB are from the *New American Standard Bible*.
Copyright © The Lockman Foundation, 1960, 1962, 1963, 1971, 1972, 1973, 1975.
Used by permission. Subsequent quotations are marked NASB.

Passages not marked NASB are the author's translation.

Dewey Decimal Classification: 232
Subject heading: JESUS CHRIST — SERMONS
Library of Congress Catalog Card Number: 79-52029
Printed in the United States of America

To my Wife
Florene
and
To my Children
Charissa
and
Craig

Who are a constant source of
Love
Encouragement
and
Strength

This book is lovingly dedicated

Foreword

What is there to write about the person and work of our Lord that has not been written many times in words more eloquent than mine? Surely very little at best. Maybe there is a new way of expressing an old truth, but there is little, if any, new light to shed on such an ancient and venerated subject. Why try then? one might ask. Simply because these thoughts have been like a fire burning within and clamoring for expression. This volume represents my small tribute to the greatness of our Lord and to that work of eternal significance which he has accomplished for all mankind.

That area of New Testament study which is called Christology and which deals with the person and work of our Lord basically asks two questions concerning him. Who is Christ? What did he do? Generally this study is arranged around various titles for our Lord which usually have to do with some function which he performed. A vast amount of technical material has been written concerning this subject by competent New Testament scholars. My purpose in writing this little book has not been to produce another technical work, but rather to produce a readable primer on Christology for the layman. Whether or not I have succeeded remains to be seen. I have tried to keep technical material and jargon to a minimum, and I have attempted to make the material palatable by interspersing illustrative material where possible.

My prayer for this little volume is that it will increase the reader's appreciation for the broad spectrum of material that relates to our Lord's person and work. If this is accomplished in any small measure, the labor will have been rewarded. There is no claim that the titles used exhaust those that relate to the area of Christology, but it is my hope that they are somewhat representative of the field.

The New Testament passages quoted at the beginning of each chapter, as well as those in the body of the material, represent my own translation from the Greek text. The Greek text used is the third edition of the United Bible Societies' Greek New Testament. All Old Testament quotations are from the *New American Standard Bible* unless otherwise indicated.

I would be remiss indeed if I did not express in some measure my appreciation to those who have given help and encouragement during the writing of this volume. My student secretary Mrs. Kathy Carden has gone the second mile in typing and retyping the manuscript. My colleagues and friends Drs. Billy K. Smith and Harold Bryson have offered help and encouragement along the way by reading parts of the manuscript and offering helpful suggestions.

I wish also to thank my family for their willingness to allow me to be absent from them on occasion during the preparation of this manuscript.

Though I have gleaned much information from many sources through the years, I have not always been able to give credit where credit may have been due. I am appreciative for the insights that have come from others during the past years of study, but ultimately the responsibility for what has been written here is my own. If there is any praise or any glory to be given, let it be given to him who is the theme of this book and who alone is worthy of our praise.

BILLY E. SIMMONS

Contents

 1 The Son of David   11
 2 The Shepherd   19
 3 The Light of the World   25
 4 He Is the One Who Emptied Himself   31
 5 The Great High Priest   39
 6 The Eternal Word   49
 7 The Preeminent One   57
 8 The One Through Whom God Speaks   63
 9 The True Vine   67
10 Savior   73
11 The Image of God   79
12 Lord   85
13 Son of Man   93
14 The Promised Seed of Abraham 103
15 The Coming Judge 109
16 The Great I Am 115
17 A Prophet Like Moses 121
18 Victor 125

1
The Son of David

The book of the genealogy of Jesus Christ, Son of David (Matt. 1:1).

And they came to Jericho. And as they were going out from Jericho with his disciples as well as a great throng, the son of Timaeus named Bartimaeus, a blind beggar was sitting beside the road. And when he heard that it was Jesus the Nazarene, he began to cry out and to say: "Jesus son of David, have mercy on me." And many were saying to him harshly that he should be quiet. But he began to cry out more, "Son of David, have mercy on me." And Jesus stopped and said: "Call him." And they called the blind man saying to him: "Take courage, arise, he calls you." And casting aside his cloak, he jumped up and came to Jesus. And Jesus making answer to him said: "What do you wish that I should do?" And the blind man said to him: "Rabboni, just to see again." And Jesus said to him: "Go, your faith has saved you." And immediately he received his sight and followed him in the way (Mark 10:46-52).

Nestled among the green foliage of a desert oasis in the great Jordan rift is the village of Jericho. For centuries this oasis had provided rest and sustenance for the weary desert traveler. The wealthier citizens of Palestine owned winter homes here because of the warm climate.

On his final journey to Jerusalem from Galilee, Jesus passed through Jericho. As he was leaving the city, headed for Jerusalem, he was confronted by the plaintive cry of a blind beggar named

Bartimaeus. "Jesus, Son of David, have mercy on me!" Though the crowd rebuked him, he continued to cry out.

What significance did the title "Son of David" have for this blind man, and why did he apply it to Jesus?

Old Testament Roots

The concept that Messiah was to be of the lineage of David finds its roots deep in the Old Testament. In 2 Samuel 7 it is recorded that because David was a man of war God would not permit him to build a house of worship. However, Samuel assured David in verse 16 that God would establish his kingdom forever. This oracle became the basis for the hope that Messiah would be of David's lineage.

After his death and during the days of the divided kingdom, David was remembered as the ideal king who had experienced God's love and guidance in a special way and lived according to God's will. His feats of heroism as shepherd, warrior, and king were remembered and chronicled in the historical literature of Israel. The great prophets of Israel looked toward the coming of the scion of the house of David who would restore Israel to her former greatness. In Isaiah 9:7, Jeremiah 23:5, Ezekiel 34:23, Hosea 3:5, Amos 9:11, and Zechariah 13:1 we find the hope of a future restoration of the house of David. Though the title Son of David does not appear in the Old Testament as a messianic title, the hope for a descendant of David who would restore Israel to its former greatness was surely present. Old Testament Judaism took the statement of Nathan to David in 2 Samuel 7:16 to mean that God would raise up an anointed ruler after the likeness of David who would establish an eternal order.

Developed in Intertestamental and Rabbinic Judaism

In the literature of the Jews which arose in the period between the Old and New Testaments there is a development of the title Son of David as a messianic title. The first actual occurrence of the title is found in the Psalms of Solomon which belongs to the first century BC, and it surely grew out of the older concepts found in the Old Testament prophets such as "root of Jesse" found in Isaiah 11:10.

During the period of Syrian domination, in about 167 BC a group of Jews revolted against the Syrians. This revolt ultimately achieved religious and political freedom for the Jews. The ruling family during this era was known as the Hasmonaeans or Maccabeans. Because of the religious confusion caused by the Syrians, these Maccabean rulers took for themselves the offices of king and priest.

There was a disillusionment among certain of the pious Jews who watched as these Maccabean kings took for themselves the office of high priest and king even though they were not of Davidic descent. When this ruling house lost independence to the Romans in 63 BC, there arose again the hope among the pious Jews that the "Son of David" would arise and deliver the Jews from Roman control.

This hope is found to be especially strong in the Dead Sea Scrolls. Though there is strong evidence that the Dead Sea community looked for two Messiahs, one of priestly lineage, the Davidic Messiah was the one who would regain political freedom for the Jewish people. The priestly Messiah was to restore proper rituals in the Temple worship.

In the prayers which pious Jews recited daily, called the "Prayer of Eighteen Benedictions," the fifteenth benediction contains this statement "May the shoot of David sprout forth quickly, and may his horn be lifted up by thy help." In the prayers called Musaph Prayers one of the blessings asked for is the "sprouting forth of a horn of David, thy servant," and the "setting up of a light for the son of Jesse, thine anointed."

The primary concept for Messiah as Son of David among the Jews of Jesus' day was that of a political strong man who would raise an army, overthrow the Romans, and establish the Davidic kingdom once more.

Jesus As Son of David

In all of the recorded sayings of Jesus there is not one instance where he referred to himself by the title Son of David. The reason for this is the obvious political overtones generated by this title. Jesus did not come to be a political deliverer. Though he was offered the opportunity to take this path more than once in his life, he steadfastly refused. In John 6:15 there is an indication that the multitudes were so impressed by the miraculous feeding that they were about to make Jesus a king by force. When Jesus sensed what they were about to do, he withdrew to the mountains to be alone. Doubtless he retreated for prayer and fellowship with the Father. He knew the purpose for which he had come into the world would be thwarted if he allowed the people to force a political role upon him in any measure.

Of the four Gospels, Matthew recorded by far the most instances of the use of the title. Undoubtedly one of Matthew's special purposes was to demonstrate that Jesus was the true Son of David. He declared this in the opening statement of his Gospel and proceeded to demonstrate it by means of his genealogy. In fact some commentators argue that by the division of the genealogy into three sections of fourteen generations each, Matthew meant to construct an acrostic on the title Son of David. For when the Hebrew letters in David's name are given their numerical equivalents, they add up to fourteen.

In Luke's Gospel record it is affirmed that Joseph with Mary went to Bethlehem for the enrollment because he was of the "house and family of David" (Luke 2:4). However, Luke did not stress the Davidic lineage as did Matthew.

Though Jesus never directly applied the title to himself and apparently did not welcome it, there are several recorded instances when it was used of him. Luke and Mark recorded only two. Matthew, on the other hand, recorded six instances when the title was used of Jesus other than the opening statement of his Gospel.

Twice (Matt. 9:27 and 20:30) blind men called out to him by this title, and each time, though he did not respond immediately, he did receive them and grant their request to have their sight restored.

In Matthew 12:23, after a healing miracle, the multitudes asked concerning him: "This one cannot be the Son of David can he?" They saw his mightly works and were impressed, but Jesus had not made himself available for the political goals of the Zealots, so there was a question concerning his identity and mission in the minds of the multitudes.

One of the most difficult of the occurrences of this title is found in Matthew 15:22 on the lips of a Canaanite woman. All of the other instances where the title is found in the gospel record it is on the lips of Jews. Here we find it on the lips of a Gentile woman. Possibly, through her contacts with Jews who were impressed with Jesus' miraculous powers, she had heard also of the messianic hope that was latent in the title. Whatever the case she surely recognized in Jesus one who was able to meet her needs. Though Jesus did not respond to her immediately, he received and responded to her need.

When Jesus entered Jerusalem at the beginning of Passion Week, the crowds responded with shouts of praise and called him "Son of David" (Matt. 21:9). Surely they recognized the Jewish imagery of his coming into Jerusalem as King to visit his subjects in peace. First Kings 1:1-40 records the importance of the mule as a royal animal among the ancient Jews. Only the king rode upon the royal mule. Thus, when Solomon was seen on David's mule, the people knew he was David's personal choice to succeed him as king. When Jesus entered Jerusalem riding upon the colt of a donkey with the mother at his side, the people knew that he was dramatizing the point that he was indeed their king. When the crowds hailed him as "Son of David," they looked upon him as the political strong man who would overthrow the Romans and set up a Davidic kingdom with Jerusalem as his capital city. There was a festive air of excitement surrounding his entry into the city. Passover was at hand and many pilgrims were already in the city for the celebration. What an opportune time for Messiah to show his strength by expelling the Romans from the land and setting up the throne of David. However, when the fickle crowd came to understand that he had no intention of overthrowing the Romans, they forsook him and demanded that he be crucified.

Jesus did not reject the title outright, but by his actions he did reject it. However, on one or two occasions he seemed to give his approval to the use of the title. In Matthew 21:15, shortly after his entry into Jerusalem, Matthew recorded the saying on the lips of children in the Temple. The chief priests and scribes became indignant. In verse 16 they asked: "Do you hear what these are saying?" In other words they wanted to know if Jesus was actually going to accept this messianic title. He answered the scribes' question by saying: "Yes; have you never read, 'Out of the mouth of infants and nursing babies you have prepared praise for yourself'?" Whether or not he accepted the title here or was merely defending the right of children to praise his act of cleansing the Temple is not readily apparent. If he did accept the title, this is the only place in the gospel record where he actually received it gladly.

As I have said several times, Jesus did not use the title of himself, but in a discussion presumably with scribes, as he taught in the Temple, he did use the title. This incident is recorded in Mark 12:35-37. Jesus began with a question: "How can the scribes say that the Christ is the son of David?" Then he continued by quoting Psalm 110:1. He concluded by saying: "David himself calls him 'Lord'; then how is he his son?" In this way he confounded the scribes and delighted the common people.

Jesus was not denying his Davidic descent according to the flesh here, but was enlarging upon the understanding of the rabbis concerning the Davidic Messiah. The Messiah was not just David's son; he was also David's Lord. The scribes looked for a worldly strong man who would overthrow the Romans and set up an earthly kingdom like that of David. Jesus affirmed that Messiah was indeed

David's son, but he was more. The popular concept of Son of David was inadequate to describe what Jesus came to do as Messiah. According to the flesh, Jesus was David's son, but in truth he was David's Lord.

2

The Shepherd

Now when Jesus was born in Bethlehem of Judea in the days of Herod the King, Behold magi from the east came to Jerusalem saying, "Where is the one who has been born King of the Jews? For we have seen his star in the east, and we have come to worship him." Now when Herod the King heard this he was troubled and all Jerusalem along with him, and he called all of the chief priests and scribes of the people and inquired from them where Christ should be born. Now they said to him in Bethlehem of Judah. For thus it stands written in the prophets; "And you, Bethlehem of Judah, are not the least among the princes of Judah. For out of you shall come a ruler, who shall shepherd my people Israel" (Matt. 2:1-6).

The figure of the shepherd is prominent in Israel's history. Often the people are likened to a flock, and God is pictured as their shepherd. Psalm 23 begins with the words "The Lord is my shepherd." In Psalm 79:13 (NASB) we read "We . . . the sheep of Thy pasture/Will give thanks to Thee forever."

On occasion the messianic hope is expressed in terms of the shepherd figure. Ezekiel spoke for God when he said: "I will set over them one shepherd, My servant David, and he will feed them; he will feed them himself and be their shepherd" (Ezek. 34:23, NASB).

The leaders of Israel were often referred to as shepherds over the flock of God. When they were unfaithful to their task, they stood under the judgment of God. We find a scathing statement of judgment in Jeremiah 23:1. " 'Woe to the shepherds who are destroying and scattering the sheep of My pasture!' declares the Lord" (NASB).

The literature of Israel is replete with picturesque characterizations concerning the shepherd and the sheep. This probably is due to the fact that the culture of Israel in the Old Testament was basically pastoral and the shepherd and his sheep were common sights throughout the land.

In the New Testament there are not nearly as many references of this sort, but the shepherd figure was a ready analogy for Jesus to use in his ministry. He used the figure in his teaching several times. In Matthew 18:12-14 he illustrated God's concern for people with the analogy of the man who had a hundred sheep and one was lost. Because of his concern for his lost sheep the man would leave the ninety-nine and search for the lost one.

In Matthew 25:32 our Lord pictured God in his role as judge performing the duty of a shepherd as he separated the sheep from the goats.

Our Lord made an indirect reference to himself as shepherd in Matthew 26:31. There he quoted Zechariah 13:7 in reference to his death. He told his disciples that they would forsake him because of this prophecy: "I will strike down the shepherd, and the sheep of the flock shall be scattered."

Peter referred to Jesus as the "shepherd of our souls" in 1 Peter 2:25. The author of the letter to the Hebrews called him "the great shepherd of the sheep" in Hebrews 13:20.

Jesus said to his followers one day: "Do not be afraid, little flock, for your Father has chosen gladly to give you the kingdom" (Luke 12:32). By the use of the term "little flock" to describe his readers, he was implicitly saying that he was their shepherd.

In John 10:1-14 we find the most detailed statement concerning our Lord as shepherd. There he gave a beautiful description of his work as shepherd and referred to himself by several terms which related to the function of the first-century Palestinian shepherd.

In verses 1-5 of John 10, Jesus used an analogy that was quite accurate in its details of the function of the shepherd:

> Truly, truly, I say to you, he who does not enter by the door into the fold of the sheep, but climbs up some other way, he is a thief and a robber. But he who enters by the door is a shepherd of the sheep. To him the doorkeeper opens; and the sheep hear his voice; and he calls his own sheep by name, and leads them out. When he puts forth all his own, he goes before them, and the sheep follow him because they know his voice. And a stranger they simply will not follow, but will flee from him, because they do not know the voice of strangers (John 10:1-5, NASB).

In ancient Israel the shepherd and his sheep faced constant peril from wild animals as well as from robbers. Often several shepherds would pool their flocks in one fold during the night. The fold might be a cave on a hillside, or it might be an area enclosed by a wall made of stones or limbs and brush. Whatever materials were used for the fold, there was always only one opening through which the sheep could pass. At night one of the shepherds lay across the opening so that no sheep could get out without disturbing him. A robber might climb over the wall, but the shepherd entered through the door. The doorkeeper of John 10 was one of several shepherds who had pooled their flocks in a single fold for additional safety.

There are numerous illustrations to be found in literature relating to Palestine that concern a shepherd and his sheep. In the Western world sheep are raised in large numbers for wool and meat. The owner of the sheep seldom has any personal attachment to the animals. In Palestine the animals were raised, not for meat, but for their wool and milk. The shepherd might not have more than a dozen sheep in his flock, and he would be with them almost constantly for the entire lifetime of the sheep. Therefore each sheep was given a name and the shepherd knew the sheep as individual animals. Beyond that each shepherd had a certain tonal quality to his voice and a peculiar call that was recognizable to his sheep. When I was a student in seminary, there was a certain professor who had been a missionary in Palestine for several years. He delighted to tell of his experiences with the Palestinian shepherds. He told of trying to fool the sheep of particular shepherds. He would go so far as to borrow the shepherd's robe and head scarf and to mimic the shepherd's peculiar call. The sheep would not respond to his call, but, when the true shepherd spoke to them, they responded without hesitation.

If several shepherds had their flocks quartered in one fold at night, there was never a problem in getting the various flocks confused. The shepherds simply came out one at a time. Each one called his flock from the fold at daybreak with his peculiar call. The sheep from other flocks never became confused for they would not respond to the call of one who was not their shepherd.

When our Lord used this analogy, his disciples were familiar with these facts, but they were unable to transfer the truth involved to Jesus. Therefore he clarified his intention by the following discourse concerning himself as the good shepherd.

Jesus therefore said to them again, "Truly, truly, I say to you, I am the door of the sheep. All who came before Me are thieves and robbers; but the sheep did not hear them. I am the door; if anyone enters through Me, he shall be saved, and shall go in and out, and find pasture. The thief comes only to steal, and kill, and destroy; I came that they might have life, and might have it abundantly. I am the good shepherd; the good shepherd lays down His life for the sheep. He who is a hireling, and not a shepherd, who is not the owner of the sheep, beholds the wolf coming, and leaves the sheep, and flees, and the wolf snatches them, and scatters them. He flees because he is a hireling, and is not concerned about the sheep. I am the good shepherd; and I know My own, and My own know me (John 10:7-14, NASB).

The first analogy which Jesus used in this passage that has relevance for his function as shepherd is that of the "door of the sheep." As I pointed out earlier, one of the shepherds would lie down in the opening to the fold, so that anyone entering or leaving the fold had to step over him. As our Shepherd, Jesus is the door through which we enter into the fold of God. All others who have made messianic claims are to be seen as thieves and robbers. They were not successful in disturbing God's fold, for the sheep would not hear them. The thief has but one intention and that is to plunder the flock. The shepherd desires to nurture and give life to the sheep.

The good shepherd was willing to lay down his life for his sheep. We are told in the Old Testament that, when King David was a shepherd lad tending his father's sheep, he fought wild beasts such as the lion and bear to defend his sheep. The shepherd was so attached to his flock that he would actually lay his life on the line in defending his sheep against wild animals and robbers. Our Lord was not speaking metaphorically here, for as you know he did lay down his life for his sheep.

There were times when the person who owned a flock of sheep could not go out into the fields with them. When this was the case, he would hire someone to go into the fields with them. The hireling would not have the same care for the flock as the one who owned them. When danger came, he would not be willing to lay his life on the line for the safety of the sheep. When robbers or wild animals attacked, he would run away, leaving the sheep at the mercy of the intruder. Jesus wanted his followers to know there was a comparison to be made between his care for his people as the good shepherd and the attitude of the hireling. He wanted to assure them of his genuine concern for them, and he did so by reaffirming the fact that he was the good shepherd. He came in strength and courage to show men and women the concern of God for them. He promised that his care and concern for his people would extend even beyond the limits of time. Thus he watches over us continually until the end of the world. Like the good shepherd he deals gently with us in our weakness and comforts us in our sorrow. As the good shepherd leads his flock to green pastures and still water, so he provides us with the bread of heaven and the water of life. Because of this we can sing:

> Savior, like a shepherd lead us,
> Much we need thy tender care;
> In thy pleasant pastures feed us,
> For our use thy folds prepare.

> Dorothy Thrupp

3
The Light of the World

Again, therefore, Jesus spoke to them saying: "I am the light of the world. The one who follows me shall never walk in darkness, but shall have the light of life" (John 8:12).

While I am in the world, I am the light of the world (John 9:5).

I have come as a light unto the world, so that those who believe in me should not remain in darkness (John 12:46).

Since very ancient times light has been associated with that which is good and darkness with that which is evil. In many of the religions of the world these categories are quite important. For instance in Zoroastrianism, the religion of Persia, the categories of light and darkness are considered to be primary forces in the world. The whole universe is the scene of a gigantic power struggle between the forces of light and the forces of darkness. Man must come to terms with these forces and make a decision for one or the other power in this struggle.

The mystics of the Greco-Roman world actually made light and God identical. In the Hermetic literature (the body of writings attributed to Hermes Trismegistus) there are many references which attribute personality and deity to light.

Though the Bible never gave personality to light, God is spoken of as light to his people. In Psalm 27:1 we find: "The Lord is my light and my salvation."

The hoped for Messiah was also said to have the quality of light. In Isaiah 42:6 God was commissioning his servant, the Messiah, and he said: "And I will appoint you as a covenant to the people,/As a light to the nations." Almost the same words are used again in Isaiah 49:6 to describe the function of the Servant of the Lord.

The categories of light and darkness are perhaps more pronounced in the literature of the Dead Sea community than in any other Jewish literature. Particularly is this true in the War Scroll. The title the community gave to this scroll was "The War Between the Sons of Light and the Sons of Darkness." The "Sons of Light" were the people of God and the "Sons of Darkness" were those belonging to the evil one. The battle which the scroll portrayed was that of the messianic conflict signaling the end of the age.

One can turn to almost any literature which serves as a background to the New Testament and find these categories of light and darkness. Light always is related to the good and to God. Though Jesus may not have had any of these ideas specifically in mind when he made his dramatic statements in the Gospel of John, the background may give aid in understanding his assertion. Three times in the Fourth Gospel Jesus asserted that he was the Light of the world (John 8:12; 9:5; 12:46). We will have more to say about these in a moment.

For the fourth evangelist the categories of light and darkness were important. Light referred to good and darkness to evil. In the first chapter John described the coming of the eternal Word into the world, and he said: "In Him was life; and the life was the light of men. And the light shines in the darkness; and the darkness did not comprehend it" (John 1:4-5, NASB). The eternal word of course came into the world in the person of Jesus Christ, and so the assertion is that one of the functions of our Savior was to be life and light for men.

In John 8:12 Jesus made a dramatic statement to the throngs gathered in the Temple area for the ceremony of the Feast of Tabernacles. The setting according to John 8:20 was in the treasury which was located in the court of women. The Feast of Tabernacles was held to commemorate the wilderness wanderings of the Israelites. During the week of this feast the men and boys built booths and slept in them at night. On the last evening of the feast the throngs gathered in the court of women. When darkness fell, the great candelabra was lighted to symbolize the pillar of fire which accompanied the Israelites on their wilderness journey. As you recall, the pillar of cloud by day became a pillar of fire by night. This was called the cloud of the presence, and later rabbis came to refer to it by the Aramaic word *Shekina,* which means presence. At this dramatic moment, when the candelabra was lighted and darkness was dispelled, when all of the throng had their minds turned to the wilderness cloud of presence, Jesus made his dramatic proclamation to the people.

John 9:5 records another occasion when Jesus proclaimed himself to be the light of the world. Just prior to giving sight to the man who was blind from birth, he declared: "While I am in the world, I am the light of the world." As soon as he said this, he performed the miracle of giving sight to the blind man.

On one other occasion Jesus declared himself to be the light of the world. In John 12:46, after he had foretold his death, he said: "I have come as light into the world, that everyone who believes in me may not remain in darkness."

Each of these statements made by our Savior had specific relevance for a particular moment in his ministry. There are, however, some general assertions that can be made in relation to his function as the light of the world.

1. Things cannot be hidden in light. Where there is light there is revelation not hiddenness. When Jesus comes, things are seen in their true light. When Jesus comes into our lives, we see ourselves as we really are and not as we think we might be. He opens our eyes to the truth about ourselves, about others, and about God. Men whose deeds are evil shun Jesus because they do not want to be seen for what they really are.

2. When light is present, one can see the way. Jesus is the light that shows us the way to God. Only through him can one truly come to know God. As that light comes into our lives, we are to be guides for others to come to him. This story came out of China when the Inland China Mission was still in operation. An old man came to the mission hospital for help. For over fifty years he had been blinded from cataracts. The doctors performed surgery and fitted him with lenses so that his sight was partially restored. One day the staff discovered that the old man had left the hospital compound. Some weeks later, as the story goes, he returned from his home province to the hospital. Those who told the story said that the old man had a long rope over his shoulder, and holding onto that rope were several other old men who were blind. The old man had gone home and had brought back with him every other old blind man who would listen to his story. He was bringing them to the source of sight. Jesus is the source of our light, and we ought to be bringing others to him.

3. Light illuminates. Even the most familiar paths become difficult to follow in the darkness. If you have ever been in a forest at night, you know that even the most familiar landmarks are difficult to identify. However, if one has a light, the path can be followed and the landmarks identified much easier.

Our Lord illuminates the pathway of life so that we can find our way through the labyrinth of difficulties and problems that constantly confront us. How much more difficult is life for the individual who does not have the Light of the world to illuminate the way.

4. Even light has its limits. Jesus reminded his followers of the need to work during the daylight hours. He said: "Night is coming, when no man can work" (John 9:4, NASB). Just as night limits day, so also does death limit life on this earth. If we are to allow the Light of the world to illumine our pathway, we must do so while we are in this world. When death overtakes our fleshly existence, we will not have an opportunity to accept the light that God has offered to us while we

were in the flesh. We must accept his offer in this life if it is to profit us in the life to come. To this extent the Light of God is limited.

5. Light and growth are corollaries. In the world of plants and animals, there can be no appreciable growth without light. If you do not believe this is so, try planting a vegetable garden where very little light from the sun can strike it. The plants will be scrawny, emaciated, and spindly. For good health and normal growth men and animals need to be exposed to the light of the sun.

This principle of life and growth is just the same in the spiritual realm. In John 1:4 we read: "In him was life; and the life was the light of men." Without proper exposure to the Light of the world, there can be no spiritual life. Without constant nourishment from this source of life there can be no significant spiritual growth.

There are many today who name the name of Christ whose growth has been retarded because they have not nourished themselves upon the source of all spiritual life. Their lives are a bane instead of a blessing. They merely exist in the limbo of a spiritual never-never land because they have not grownup unto Christ. They have remained spiritual babes who know nothing of the solid food of spiritual maturity. If we are to grow as we should, we must remain close to the source of our spiritual life—the Light of the world.

6. There is strength in light. In John 1:5 we find this statement: "And the light shines in the darkness; and the darkness did not comprehend it." The word translated "comprehend" contains the idea of overcome rather than understand. John did not intend to say that the darkness did not understand the light but that the darkness did not overcome the light.

Goodness will ultimately triumph over evil. The forces of God will be victorious over the forces of the devil. As we walk life's pathway during our little day, it may appear that evil does indeed have the upper hand. We must remember, however, that our three score years and ten do not give us a true perspective of the vast plane of redemptive history. One battle does not necessarily win a war, and our perspective is severely limited to our immediate era. God is in control of history and through Jesus Christ has won the victory that will one day be underscored by the banishment of the forces of evil with all their followers.

4

He Is the One Who
Emptied Himself

*Continue to cultivate the same mental attitude for yourselves
which was evident in Christ Jesus, who had his permanent existence
in the form of deity but did not consider being on an equality with
God a thing to which he should cling but he emptied himself taking
the form of a slave, becoming in the likeness of men; and being found
fashioned as a man he humbled himself becoming obedient until the
very point of death, even the death of the cross. On the basis of this,
God highly exalted him and granted to him the name which is above
every name, so that at the name of Jesus every knee should bow,
whether heavenly beings, earthly beings or subterranean beings, and
every tongue shall confess that Jesus Christ is Lord to the glory of
God the Father* (Phil. 2:5-11).

There have been times in the history of mankind when significant
happenings have been produced by seemingly insignificant causes. It
is said that Newton was able to define the law of gravity because an
apple falling from a tree struck him on the head. Benjamin Franklin
supposedly realized the potential for harnessing electricity while
flying a kite during a thunderstorm. In this case a slight discord in an
obscure church became the occasion for one of Paul's most eloquent
statements concerning his conception of the person of Christ. It may
have been the misunderstanding between Euodia and Syntyche
(Phil. 4:2) which prompted this beautiful hymn. At any rate, it is upon
this statement that Paul based his inspiring appeal for Christians to
imitate Christ. The implication is that harmony and unity within the

Christian community can be achieved only to the extent that believers are willing to submit themselves to one another in this same spirit of humility.

In this majestic hymn to Christ Paul has drawn back the veil of eternity to give the reader a glimpse of the grandeur of the preincarnate state of the eternal Christ. Then he moves incisively through the humility which was his in the incarnation. And he concludes by pointing to the eschatological glorification that can belong only to the Lord Christ.

The Challenge (v. 5)

Paul's clarion call to imitate Christ is really presented in the form of a challenge. Though the form of the verb might indicate a mere appeal, there is good reason to see it as a challenge. There is a sense of urgency in the context which seems to demand that the verb form be taken as an imperative.

The word which Paul used for mind connotes more the idea of a mental attitude or disposition than the actual thinking processes. This same word was used by Paul in Philippians 1:7 when he said: "It is only right for me to *feel* this way about all of you." He also used it in Colossians 3:2 where he admonished his readers to "*set your mind* on things which are above." Therefore Paul was exhorting the Philippian Christians to cultivate the same attitude or mental disposition that their Lord displayed when he was in the flesh.

For some Christians, the imitation of Christ involves an attempt to imagine what Christ would do under certain circumstances and then to do it. For Paul, the true imitation of Christ consisted in cultivating the spirit and the disposition of Christ. This ought to be the Christian's way of facing the world. When the mind of Christ is cultivated, the Christian will not have to stop and ask himself "What would Jesus do?" He will rather react to the situation properly because he has cultivated the proper mental disposition.

Now that Paul has challenged his readers to imitate Christ, he proceeded to graphically illustrate those qualities which marked the mind of the Master.

Preincarnate Glory (v. 6)

With the deft stroke of a master artist Paul proceeded to paint a vivid verbal picture of the glory that belonged to the cosmic Christ prior to his incarnation. An accurate paraphrase of the first part of verse 6 might be "Who had his eternal existence as one who possessed the very essence of deity."

The word Paul used to describe the eternal existence of the preincarnate Christ refers to a state of being that is continual or permanent. In other words, Paul has affirmed that our Lord was not a created being. In the aeons of eternity past the cosmic Christ was present. He did not come into being because he always has been and always will be.

His being in the glory of eternity was in the form of deity. "Form" refers to the essential attributes of a thing or a person. It usually refers to outward form and implicit in the word is the reality of the person or thing. The preincarnate Christ had real form though not necessarily physical. Some have taught that the Son had only an ideal preincarnate state. Their belief is that he existed only as an idea in the mind of God, and that the idea became a reality only when Jesus was born to Mary. This statement of Paul would strongly militate against such a heretical teaching.

His existence in his preincarnate state was that of essential deity. The noun for God occurs here without the definite article, and it is generally accepted by scholars that the occurrence of the noun without the article refers to the essence of deity, rather than to the personhood of the Father. When the article is present, the reference is to the divine personality. In other words, Paul was not confusing our Lord in his preincarnate state with the Father.

Though our Lord had his existence as perpetual deity in his preincarnate state, he did not view this as something to which he should cling. He was equal to the deity! That is to say our Lord was coeternal with God the Father, but he did not view this state as something to which he should hold tenaciously.

Self-Emptying (vv. 7-8)

Paul began this statement with a strong adversative conjunction indicating a change in the direction of his thought. He has just asserted that the preincarnate Christ did not determine that he should hold fast to the prize of essential deity. Now to describe what took place in the incarnation, Paul used a picturesque word. It is the word from which this beautiful passage gets its title. It is referred to as the *Kenosis* hymn. The word means to empty a vessel of its contents; to turn a pitcher upside down and completely pour out its contents. The derived idea, when applied to a person, is that he has completely divested himself of certain prerogatives. In other words, at the incarnation our Lord completely divested himself of the prerogatives which were his as essential deity.

The form of the verb used for the act of emptying is such that it is possible to see here a reference to Christ's entrance into the world as a babe in Bethlehem's manger. If so, this is a marvelous theological tribute to the importance of the Christmas story for the world of men. For it tells us that our Lord deigned to leave the councils of deity in realms of glory and come to earth so he might identify himself with mankind in their helpless plight.

One of the consequences of our Lord's entrance into this world as a man is reflected in Paul's assertion "he took the form of a slave." The word for form is the same here as the one used in verse 6, and it has to do with the essential nature of the person. Paul's emphasis here is on the reality of the servanthood of our Lord. It was not the sham suggested by certain heretical groups who claimed that Jesus only seemed to be a man.

Though our Lord never used the term "servant" to refer to himself, he did see this as one of his primary roles. His favorite self-designation was "Son of man," but often this title reflects the role of the suffering servant of Isaiah. For instance, in Mark 10:45 we read: "For even the Son of man did not come to be ministered to but to minister and to give his life a ransom for many."

Surely Paul was aware of this gospel tradition, and he has stated this truth succinctly. He took the form of a slave. Then, as if he wished to emphasize the reality of his humanity even further, he added the phrase "becoming in the likeness of men." This is no phantom likeness; his manhood was genuine. The verb for becoming is different both in tense and meaning from the one used to describe his existence as essential deity in verse 6. Though it is sometimes used as a substitute for the verb to be, it means to become. The tense indicates a definite point of entrance into the sphere of time and space. The Fourth Evangelist showed the same distinction when in John 1:14 he wrote "the word *became* flesh." By this construction, Paul has asserted that our Lord's incarnate state is as real as his preincarnate state though not as permanent.

Paul continues to move incisively through the incarnation by progressing toward the humiliation. By using the phrase "being found fashioned as a man" he had reference to our Lord's outward appearance. The word used for "fashioned" is the word from which our English words *scheme* and *schematic* come.

Thus humanity of our Savior was just as real as his deity though not as permanent. His humanity was real but temporary. His deity is real as well as permanent. We must not rob him of either his deity or humanity. Either is heresy. He was not part God and part man; a hybrid. He was the God-man.

Humility and Obedience (v. 8)

One of the most meaningful descriptions of the humility and sufferings of our Savior is found in the verse of Paul's majestic hymn. The phrase "he humbled himself" describes a quality of character that was degrading as far as the self-respecting Greek was concerned.

For the Greek writers, it was a term of derision, a vice rather than a virtue. A slave or perhaps a woman might display humility but never a Greek man. He was proud, arrogant, and self-sufficient, and he looked disdainfully on anyone who displayed a spirit of humility. However, the Christian writers in general and Paul in particular took this word and made it a thing of beauty, dignity, and grace. As he used it of our Lord, it is interesting to note that it does not describe something which was forced upon him. Rather it describes a quality of life which our Lord chose for himself. His was a voluntary humility or self-abasement.

In addition to this Paul affirms that our Lord became obedient. The word literally means to give ear to someone. To hear what is said, to understand it, and then to do it is the essence of this word. Throughout his incarnation our Lord was obedient to the Father. There was never a moment when he veered from the path set for him by his Father. The culmination of his life of obedience can be seen at Calvary. Not only did he forsake his existence of glorified deity for the humility of the incarnation but as a man he died. In his death he turned his back on everything that man calls glory. He rejected the fame that some would have given him as a miracle worker. He refused the kingdoms of this world when they were offered to him on the devil's terms. He accepted instead the most shameful death of his day. Crucifixion was reserved for thieves, murderers, and insurrectionists. So abhorrent was this form of death that the Old Testament pronounced a curse on anyone who died in this way (Deut. 21:23).

Our Lord was not just obedient unto death. The preposition used here indicates degree or measure. He was obedient to the very dying point. Being obedient until death may not be too difficult if death comes swiftly. However, when one is put to death by degrees, obedience can become a supreme test. Our Lord's death was a slow, painful method, and he was obedient to the very point of dying.

His Exaltation (vv. 9-11)

When the word "wherefore" appears in Paul's epistles, the reader is alerted to the fact that what follows is based on what has just been said. In other words, the assertion that Paul is about to make concerning the exaltation of our Lord is based on his humiliation and death.

There appears to be a progression in early Christian theology concerning the interpretation of Christ's sufferings. In Matthew 16:22 it is recorded that Peter rebuked Jesus for even suggesting that as the Messiah he must suffer. Later, in the early apostolic preaching in Acts, it is recorded that Peter preached that God exalted Jesus and made him both Prince and Savior in spite of his humiliating death at the hands of sinful men. (See Acts 2:36; 5:30-31.) Now as Paul penned these words to the Christians at Philippi he affirmed that Christ's exaltation is based on his humiliation.

"God highly exalted him." The definite article is present; therefore the reference is to God the Father. Jesus has been supremely exalted by the fact that he has been granted the name which is above every name. What is that name? Is it the name Jesus which means Savior? The proximity of the name Jesus in verse 11 would appear to lend credence to that view. There are others who maintain that Paul had the exalted title Lord in mind. Still others opt for the ineffable name of God in the Old Testament. That name which was written but never spoken for fear that the name of God might be taken in vain. There is no way to know exactly what name Paul had in mind, but we can be sure that it is an exalted one.

The result of his exaltation is that every knee shall bow before him and every tongue will confess that he is Lord. Paul was most inclusive in his reference: "whether heavenly beings, earthly beings, or subterranean beings." This will all be done to bring glory to God the Father.

Our spiritual legacy would be much the poorer had Paul not

exhorted the membership of this obscure New Testament congregation to imitate the Lord Christ. Paul's immediate goal in writing this may have been to quell the Philippian church, but the glorious result is one of the most sublime statements concerning the person and work of Christ in all of the New Testament.

5

The Great High Priest

Having therefore a great high priest who has passed through the heavens, Jesus the Son of God, let us hold fast our confession. For we do not have a high priest who cannot sympathize with our weakness, but one who has been tempted in all points like we are yet without sin. Let us draw near therefore with boldness to the throne of grace; so that we might receive mercy and may find grace that is helpful coming at the time of our need (Heb. 4:14-16).

The Background

The only New Testament document that refers to Jesus by the title High Priest is the letter to the Hebrews. What was there about the person and work of our Lord that caused this writer to refer to him by this title when no other New Testament writer used it? Is there any historical precedent for such a title for Messiah? If there is, why was this writer the only one to make use of it? These are questions that have occupied the minds of New Testament scholars for years.

Many New Testament scholars recognize no Old Testament background for this concept at all. There are, however, some Old Testament passages which certainly are related to the argument as set forth by the writer of the letter to the Hebrews. In Psalm 110:4 we find: "The Lord has sworn and will not change His mind,/'Thou art a priest forever/According to the order of Melchizedek'" (NASB). Though this verse has nothing to say about a high priestly ministry, it surely is related to it, and the writer of the letter to the Hebrews capitalized on this relationship in his argument. Psalm 110 was one of the major passages in the Old Testament which the earliest Christians accepted as messianic.

Isaiah 53:12 states that the Servant of the Lord will intercede for the transgressors. Through the title high priest is not used, intersession is surely one of the primary priestly functions. Again Isaiah 53 is a major segment of Old Testament Scripture that has been accepted as messianic by Christians since the earliest days.

There are several other Old Testament passages that relate to a priestly function for the coming Messiah. Perhaps the most significant of these is found in Malachi 3:1-3. In this passage the prophet speaks of the messenger of the Lord coming to cleanse the Temple. Beyond that he will purify the sons of Levi. There surely is more than a hint here that the Messiah's function was to be a priestly one.

In the intertestamental literature there is some evidence of the hope for a priestly Messiah. The work called the *Testament of the Twelve Patriarchs* certainly reflects such a hope. In the Testament of Levi we find that the Messiah is to be a priest-king of the tribe of Levi. Though we know that our Lord is of the tribe of Judah, it is significant that there was hope for a priestly Messiah among some Jews.

The documents from the Dead Sea community of Qumran also reflect the hope for a priestly Messiah. In the War Scroll entitled *The War Between the Sons of Light and the Sons of Darkness,* the final struggle between the forces of good and evil is described. The messianic banquet is also described and the protocol for it is given. Two Messiahs are mentioned. One is a descendant of David and he is the leader of the army. Another is a descendant of Levi, and his function is that of priest. The Davidic Messiah institutes temporal rule and the priestly Messiah restores the proper sacrificial rituals in the temple.

Jesus As High Priest in the New Testament

When our Lord came in the flesh, he was not born into a family with a priestly ancestry, as a glance at his genealogy will show. There is no evidence that he had any desire to function as a priest in cultic Judaism. However, he did show revulsion for the practice of the priestly cult in Jerusalem as his act of cleansing the Temple clearly demonstrates. He also conceived of his work as a sacrificial one as the ransom saying of Mark 10:45 shows. Also in Mark 12:35-36 Jesus quoted Psalm 110:1 and applied it to the Messiah. Though it is true that he did not quote verse 4 which deals with the priestly function, the fact that he quoted from the psalm is an indication that he thought of it as messianic.

Though no New Testament writer other than the author of Hebrews referred to our Lord by the title High Priest, there are several instances where his priestly work is alluded to. Our Lord's intercessory and mediatorial work are referred to several times in the epistles of Paul as well as the other New Testament documents. His sacrificial death is the theme about which much of the New Testament revolves. Certainly these ideas are a genuine part of his work as High Priest.

As is well known, the primary emphasis of the letter to the Hebrews is the development of the argument for Jesus as High Priest. The writer was intent on proving that Jesus is superior to everything in the old Jewish economy. He is superior to the prophets, to angels, to Moses, and ultimately to the Jewish priesthood. He developed his argument around Psalm 110:4: "The Lord has sworn and will not change his mind,/'Thou art a priest forever/According to the order of Melchizedek' " (NASB). As a priest after the order of Melchizedek, Jesus is superior to the Levitical priesthood. Beyond this the writer argued that our Lord's priestly work was done in the realm of the eternal and the true, whereas the Levitical priests accomplished their work in the realm of the temporal and the shadow. The work of the earthly high priests had to be repeated often; our Lord's priestly work was done once for all. The earthly priests worked with the blood of animals. Our Lord offered his own blood, shed for the sins of mankind. The work of the earthly priests provided ritual cleansing from sins committed in ignorance for one year. Our Lord's sacrifice provides complete cleansing from all sins for all time.

The Significance of Christ's Work As High Priest

In viewing the priestly work of our Lord there are three distinct phases to which we should give our attention. (1) As our High Priest, he brings God to man in his own person. (2) He brings man to God in his own person, and (3) his priesthood extends into the life of every believer.

He Brings God to Man

In seeking to understand his function of bringing God to man we may focus our attention on his work as mediator. This term is used of Jesus four times in the New Testament, and three of them are found in the letter to the Hebrews. Generally speaking, a mediator is one who can represent two other parties, often during times of a dispute. For our purposes a mediator is one who can represent God to men and represent men to God, thus bringing them together. Though this title could conceivably be used of bringing man to God, in the New Testament the work of Christ as mediator is centered in our Lord's work as God's representative to men.

By examining the three passages in Hebrews where the word *mediator* is used of Christ, one can easily see that this title is applied to our Lord in his work as High Priest. In Hebrews 8:6 it is said that Christ is "the mediator of a better covenant." In 9:15 he is called the "mediator of a new covenant." In each of these contexts his work as High Priest is quite prominent in the author's mind.

In Hebrews, Christ's mediatorial work is always linked with the new or better covenant which is brought into being by his sacrificial death. The writer explained this new or better covenant in terms of the old covenant. When the first or the old covenant came into being, Moses was the mediator. Paul made this clear in Galatians 3:19-20.

However, God's own Son is the mediator of the new covenant, and because of this, it is superior to the old covenant in every way. That the author of the letter to the Hebrews was steeped in the Old Testament is evident, for the entire idea of our Lord as mediator is grounded in Old Testament concepts. He argued quite strongly that Christ's mediatorial activity is based upon his sacrifice as High Priest. He argued that it was through his own blood that Christ was able to obtain eternal redemption. It is on the basis of his sacrifice that our Lord has become the mediator of this new covenant.

The fact that Jesus' role as mediator is based on his death is important for understanding his task as mediator. The letter to the Hebrews presents our Lord as the mediator of the new covenant, dying on the cross for the purpose of obtaining eternal redemption. In other words, the writer of Hebrews recognized that God was at work in the mediatorial activity of Christ. In fact he might have said that God was in Christ mediating a new covenant just as Paul said that "God was in Christ reconciling the world unto himself" (2 Cor. 5:19). The message of the letter to the Hebrews is that it is the mediatorial work of Christ that reconciles man to God.

Our Lord's mediatorial activity finds its consummation on the cross where he gave himself a ransom for all, thus establishing a new covenant in his blood by which he obtained eternal redemption. The New Testament presents our Lord as the only one who is qualified to do the work of mediator. This is true because of his unique personality. In him very God and perfect man meet in a totally integrated personality. Because of this he can perfectly represent them both in his mediatorial activity on the cross. In his own person our Lord has overcome the distance that has existed between God and man. From the cross it is as though he reached one hand into heaven and clasped the hand of God and with the other hand he reached down to earth to clasp the hand of man thus bringing man and God together in his own person.

He Brings Man to God

The second aspect of his work of High Priest is that of bringing man to God. As our Lord through the perfections of his unique personality brings God to man, so he also brings man to God. Because of his solidarity with the human race through his incarnation, our Lord can be called the representative High Priest of humanity who brings man to God. On the ground of his solidarity with us we can say two things. (1) When Christ suffered, died, rose again, and ascended into heaven over nineteen hundred years ago, we were included in his high priestly work. We have in the person of our High Priest entered into the presence of God on the ground of his atoning work. (2) When our Lord was judged for our sins on the cross, when he rose again for our justification and ascended to be with the Father, God accepted us in him. In the person of our beloved High Priest we have entered into the presence of the Eternal and have been accepted. That is to say all of God's covenant relations with us are mediated to us in and through the person of our great High Priest.

The writer of the letter to the Hebrews used several terms which are related to this aspect of our Lord's high priestly work. In Hebrews 2:10 and 12:2 we find the term pioneer used of Jesus. Sometimes it is translated by our English word *author*. The word describes one who takes the lead in anything, thus affording an example for others who follow. The term, as it is used in Hebrews, is closely connected with our Lord's suffering and his solidarity with his people. As pioneer, our Lord has cleared the way for us into the presence of God. This is true because of his incarnation through which he is seen as being in solidarity with humanity and by his high priestly activity on the cross which resulted in his exaltation to God's right hand. He has cleared the way into the presence of God for us through his obedience and self-offering, thus making it possible for us to appropriate this obedience and self-offering for ourselves.

In Hebrews 6:20 Jesus is called the Christian's forerunner. This is the only place in the New Testament where this word is used. The word has to do with the function of going before another. The idea in the word is closely akin to the function which was performed by the scout for the westward bound wagon trains a century or more ago. Our Lord's task as forerunner is vitally connected with his function as High Priest and is closely connected with his activity as pioneer. In Hebrews 6:19 the writer indicates that it is "within the veil" that Jesus enters as our forerunner. This expression is a reference to the most holy place in the Temple which was representative of God's presence among his people. Under the old covenant only the high priest was allowed to enter the most holy place, and he did so only once a year. No other person was ever allowed within the sacred precinct which was within the veil. As our forerunner, our Lord has entered into the presence of God and beckons us to come to him there.

In Hebrews 7:25 the writer states that, because of his high priesthood, our Lord "is able to save forever those who draw near to God through Him, since He always lives to make intercession for them." The word translated intercession conveys the idea of pleading. Because of his work as High Priest, our Lord is placed in a position where he can plead for those who come to God through him. His function as our intercessor is a logical extension of his work as pioneer and forerunner. For, as our intercessor, he pleads our cause before God to make it possible for us to come into the presence of God.

Because of the perfections of his person and because of his exaltation which is based on his suffering, our Lord is able to bring man to God. This he has done beautifully as our pioneer, forerunner, and intercessor.

The Aspect of Extension

The final aspect of our Lord's high priesthood is that of extension. Though the idea of the priesthood of believers is generally recognized, it is not often seen as an extension of the high priestly work of our Lord. It is generally viewed as a privilege which the believer enjoys because of Christ's activity on his behalf and the believer's relation to Christ. However, I believe that our priesthood includes responsibility as well as privilege and that it is in a real sense an extension of our Lord's work as priest. True the priesthood is ours in a very real sense, but it belongs to us only because of what Jesus has done for us as High Priest.

Perhaps the most neglected phase of the priesthood of the believer is that of the believer's responsibility of submitting himself completely to the lordship of Christ. This concept can be seen most clearly in the New Testament in Romans 12:1-2. Because of our Lord's sacrifice on our behalf we are enabled to submit our will to God which is in effect a sacrificial act. This is a demand which Christ made upon his followers. In Matthew 16:24 we find that he said: "If anyone desires to come after me, let him deny himself and take up his cross and follow me." As the believer dies to self, he is really submitting his will to God in obedience to Christ's command. This can be done only because our Lord first died for us on the cross in obedience to the Father. Paul had this in mind when he said in Galatians 2:19b-20: "I am crucified with Christ. I live, yet not I but Christ lives in me. And the life which I now live in the flesh, I live by the faith of the Son of God who loved me and gave himself up on my behalf." In our act of self-denial we become related to that greater act of obedience and sacrifice, thus our submission is in this sense an extension of our Lord's priestly work.

Of all the privileges which the believer has because of the high priestly sacrifice of Christ, access to God is surely the greatest. The New Testament teaches that our access to God is only through the person of Jesus Christ. To put it another way, we receive the priestly right of access because of our relationship to Christ and his work as High Priest. In Hebrews 10:19-22 this concept is expressed perhaps more clearly than it is anywhere else in the New Testament.

> Since therefore, brethren, we have confidence to enter the holy
> place by the blood of Jesus, by a new and living way which He
> inaugurated for us through the veil, that is, His flesh, and since
> *we have* a great priest over the house of God, let us draw near
> with a sincere heart in full assurance of faith, having our hearts
> sprinkled *clean* from an evil conscience and our bodies washed
> with pure water.

Surely our right of access to God is based on what our Lord did for
us as High Priest and it is also an extension of his ministry.

The extension of our Lord's priestly ministry into the life of his
people involves the submission of the believer's will as well as access
to God. Beyond these, there is that aspect of sharing in the ministry
of reconciliation. Because of what Christ has done as High Priest,
there is the offer of salvation through him to all who will trust him.

To the church has been committed the task of evangelism. As we
share the good news about Jesus Christ with the world, we are
cooperating with our Lord in an extension of his own priestly work.
We have a message to share with the world only because of what our
Lord did through his death, resurrection, and exaltation. In 1 Peter
2:5 Christians are called a "holy priesthood" and in 2:9 it is said that,
as a holy priesthood, the church is to "show forth the excellencies" of
God. The context of 1 Peter 2:1-10 implies that Christians are a
priesthood because of what Christ has done, because of what our
Lord has done for us, and what he is doing in and through us. This
ministry of reconciliation is not relegated to a special group of
Christians. Rather it is the task of every Christian. Our Lord wants to
extend himself through us to the world of lost human beings, and this
is done as we share in the ministry of reconciliation.

6

The Eternal Word

In the beginning was the word, and the word was with God and the word was deity. This same one was in the beginning with God. All things were made through him, and apart from him nothing was made (John 1:1-3).

And the word became flesh and pitched his tent among us and we beheld his glory, glory as of the unique one from the Father, full of grace and truth (John 1:14).

Of all the inspired writers only John referred to Jesus by the title *logos* or Word. He did so in the prologue of the Gospel of John (1:1-18) and in the First Epistle of John (1:1).

There is a dual background for this concept. The Old Testament as well as the extrabiblical Jewish literature made use of this concept. Also this concept can be found in the Greek literature of the philosophers. For years scholars have debated as to which of these backgrounds was dominant in the mind of John when he penned these thoughts. Proponents of the Greek background point to the fact that tradition places the origin of the Gospel in Ephesus near the end of the first century. Those opting for Jewish background point to the evangelist's Jewish heritage and to the Greek translation of the Old Testament (the Septuagint) which was a ready tool for Greek-speaking Christians of the first century.

Since this issue probably will never be settled to the satisfaction of everyone and since there are two legitimate strands of historical material, we will look briefly at each.

The first Greek thinker of record to use the term *logos* in any way similar to that of John was the sixth century BC thinker Heraclitus. It may be of some significance that Heraclitus resided at Ephesus as did John the evangelist. Heraclitus saw the whole world as being in a state of flux. Everything was constantly changing. However, within this flux, he recognized a definite ordered pattern. That which gave order to the changing patterns he called the *logos*. In other words the *logos* for Heraclitus was the mind, order, or reason behind the universe.

Out of all of the schools of philosophy to be found in the Greek world perhaps the most influential group was the Stoics. Basically the Stoics were pantheists, though they liked to refer to themselves as atheists. That is they did not accept the many gods of the Greek pantheon into their system of thought. They used the term *logos* to describe the immanent reason which pervades the universe.

Philo of Alexandria, a Jewish thinker born in 20 BC, was steeped in Greek philosophy. In fact one of his avowed purposes in life was to harmonize the Hebrew Scriptures with Greek philosophy. For him the *logos* had many functions in the work of God, but he stopped short of giving divine personality to the *logos*. He spoke of the *logos* as "High Priest," "Son of God," and "First Born," but for him it was an impersonal principle.

If John were writing primarily to Greeks out of a background of Greek philosophy, he might have been saying something like this: "You have read of the *logos* in the writings of your philosophers, let me introduce you to him." In other words he may have been taking a concept which was familiar to them as a beginning, so that he could move them toward an understanding of the person and work of our Lord.

Lest we forget, however, there is also some very significant Jewish background for John's use of *logos* to refer to our Lord. For the Jews a word was not just something spoken. A word, once it was spoken, became an entity that had potential for either good or bad. In Isaiah

55:11 we find: "So shall My word be which goes forth from My mouth;/It shall not return to Me empty,/Without accomplishing what I desire,/And without succeeding in the matter for which I sent it" (NASB). In all of the creative acts of God we find the inspired writer saying: "And God said." The word was considered to be an entity that carried its own energy for the task at hand.

Often in the prophetic literature of the Old Testament we read that the word of the Lord came unto the prophet. Each time this occurred the prophet was given a message or a mission and was empowered to deliver the message or accomplish the mission.

At least once in the Old Testament the word of the Lord comes very close to receiving personality. In 1 Kings 13 an interesting account is recorded. The divided kingdom had just become a reality with Rehoboam, the son of Solomon, ruling the two tribes south and Jeroboam, the son of Nebat, ruling the ten tribes north. Jeroboam had set up shrines in the northern and southern ends of his kingdom at Dan and Bethel to consolidate his rule and to keep the people from going back to Jerusalem for the feast days. He had golden calves fashioned and placed at each shrine and he told his people that these were representatives of Jehovah. By the word of the Lord an unnamed prophet out of Judah went up to Bethel and prophesied against the shrine. This infuriated Jeroboam who was officiating as priest of the altar. He stretched out his hand toward the prophet and his arm withered. Jeroboam pled with the old prophet to ask God to restore his arm as before and he did. Then Jeroboam invited the old prophet to come home with him and refresh himself. The old prophet refused because the word of the Lord had told him not to eat bread or drink water in that place. Some brothers who had witnessed this scene told their father who was also a prophet of God about it. Desiring to have fellowship with a true prophet, he pursued the old man and asked him to return home with him. When the old prophet refused, the man lied and said that an angel had spoken to him by the word of the Lord directing him to bring the old prophet back to his home. While they were eating, the word of the Lord took control of the old man who had brought the prophet to his home and spoke through his faculties a word of judgment upon the unnamed prophet. Though the "word of the Lord" is not given personality here as in John 1, the usage is certainly striking.

In the Targums (the Aramaic interpretations of the Old Testament in sermonic form) we find the Aramaic word *memra* which answers to the Greek *logos* quite often. In fact this expression frequently was a substitute for the name as well as for the actions of God.

Scholars often point to the use of wisdom in the Old Testament (particularly in Prov. 8) as a possible background for the term *logos* in the Old Testament. It is quite true that in Proverbs 8 wisdom is very closely identified with God and is almost given personality. This usage, however, is somewhat removed from John's use of the term *logos*.

When we begin to interpret John's use of the term *logos* for our Lord, we should remember that *logos* could mean more than word. It could mean reason, principle, or even mind. However, our English translation "word" probably comes as close as any to capturing the essence of what John had in mind as do any of the others. It is as though John were saying to the Jews in his reading audience: "You have heard the rabbis speak of the Word of the Lord and you have read in the Old Testament of him; I would like to introduce you to him."

As the Word, John said that our Lord is eternal. His existence did not begin when he was born as a babe in Bethlehem's manger. Rather he was in the beginning. John made no mistake in his affirmation. The tense which he used of the verb "to be" indicates that he was saying that the Word always has been. He has had his existence in perpetual eternal being. John does not elaborate on the time frame for his existence. He merely pushed his existence back to the beginning. Whenever and wherever that was, the Word was there already existing in his perpetual eternal form. In so doing John affirmed that our Lord was not a created being. Rather he always has been and always will be.

John also affirmed that as the Eternal Word our Lord was coeternal and coexistent with God the Father. Though the word *trinity* is not found in the New Testament, the doctrine of the Triune God abounds throughout its pages. Here we are introduced to two of the persons of the Godhead. John did not confuse the Son with the Father at all. It is axiomatic in New Testament Greek that, when the definite article appears with the noun God, the divine personality is generally in mind. When the definite article does not appear, the divine essence is generally intended. At this point the definite article appears. The Word was with God the Father. Beyond this, the construction which John used indicates equality. The phrase could be translated face to face with God. In the ancient East diplomatic protocol was rigidly followed. When two monarchs met, it was essential that they be equal in every way. If one was on a higher throne, that was considered a serious breach of protocol. Therefore, if one king happened to be taller than the other, the short king's throne had to be adjusted upward so that he could look the taller king in the face. This implied equality, and the same phrase that is found in John 1:1 was used to describe this. In his preincarnate state as the Eternal Word, our Lord was in a position of equality to God the Father.

In the next statement John further elaborated on the deity of our Lord in his preincarnate state. "The Word was God" is generally the way it is translated. In this particular construction God does not have the definite article, so the translation can be: "The Word was Deity." The *New World Translation* renders it by the statement, "The Word was a god." This translation, however, is not according to the rules of good Greek grammar.

In verse 3 John used a construction which indicates agency. In other words the Eternal Word was the agent through whom God spoke worlds into being. John was quite inclusive. "All things" is a phrase that leaves nothing to chance or to the imagination. As we view the wonders of the universe, we are beholding the masterpiece of the Creator God who worked through the Eternal Word to bring it into being. To be sure there was no misunderstanding, John used a very strong negative construction to indicate that there was nothing that was made except through the creative fiat of the Eternal Word.

One of the grandest assertions concerning the Eternal Word of God is found in John 1:14. This is John's affirmation concerning the incarnation of our Lord. By the short statement "the Word became flesh," John combated a heresy that was already festering in the early church. In the second century this heresy was formalized under the name gnosticism. However, the germinal ideas of the heresy were in existence for some time before it received the name. One avenue of thought which this heresy took was to deny the fact that our Lord was flesh and blood. In other words, those who subscribed to this system of thought refused to accept the humanity of our Lord. There are still well-meaning individuals today who refuse to allow our Lord his full humanity during the days of his flesh. If we are to be true to the Scriptures, we must accept the fact that our Lord developed physically and mentally during his days from infancy as any other child develops. The verb John used for "became" in this verse is different from the one he used in verse 1 to describe his eternal being. The tense of this verb as well as its meaning stress the fact that at a definite point the Eternal Word took upon himself the limitations of flesh.

Beyond this, John tells us that he "dwelt among us" (NASB). The word for "dwelt" can be translated "tabernacled" or "pitched his tent." The verb that John used is reminiscent of the presence of God among his people Israel during their wilderness wanderings. God manifested his presence among them by a cloud by day and a pillar of fire by night. This presence cloud came to be known by the rabbis as the *Shekinah*. Though this rabbinic word means presence, it is often spoken of as the glory cloud. God's glory was manifested in the cloud of the presence as his people camped in the wilderness. That

John had this manifestation in mind may be indicated by his statement "and we beheld his glory, glory of the only begotten from the Father, full of grace and truth."

The word *glory* can also be translated brilliance or radiance. Generally in the New Testament it denotes a heavenly or divine brilliance. Sometimes it has to do with the loftiness and the majesty of God. This appears to be true in this verse, for John indicates that the glory of the Word in his incarnation is really a reflection of God's radiance. The Eternal Word has come from the Father, and because of this, he brings with him the glory that belongs peculiarly to God.

7

The Preeminent One

*And he is the head of the body, which is the church. Who is the
beginning, the first born from the dead, so that in all things he might
be preeminent* (Col. 1:18).

The heretics in Colosse had removed Christ from the central
position in their world view. He was just one of a hierarchy of
semidivine angelic beings who had to do with salvation. For them, he
was not the unique Son of God, but rather a created being. He was
not the creator and sustainer of the universe, nor was he the divine
redeemer from sin. To them he was not the Lord of the church nor
was he supreme in the believer's life. They had supplanted and
preempted his preeminence in all these areas with a multitude of
angelic beings.

Paul's answer to these heretics in the marvelous little letter to the
Colossians was a resounding rebuff. Within this epistle, we find one
of the loftiest Christological statements to be found in all of the New
Testament. The heart of this Christological statement is to be found in
verse 18, where Paul makes his statement concerning the preeminence of Christ. Hear Paul's clarion call: "That in all things he
might have preeminence." "All things" covers a vast amount of territory, but I should like to suggest four areas in which the Christian
must recognize the preeminence of Christ. I believe these four areas
were of central concern to Paul when he dictated this grand epistle to
his amanuensis. They are creation, redemption, the church, and the

Christian life. This, I believe, is the essence of the theme of Colossians.

He Was Preeminent in Creation

The heretics had declared Christ to be a created being. The New Testament declares him to be the agent of the Sovereign God in creating and sustaining the universe. John, Paul, and the author of Hebrews declared most emphatically of the New Testament writers that the Lord Christ was the creative agent when the worlds were framed. In John 1:3 we read: "All things were made through him, and without him was not anything made that was made." In Hebrews 1:2 these words are found: "But in these last days he has spoken to us by a Son, whom he appointed the heir of all things, through whom also he created the world." Then note Paul's words in Colossians 1:16: "For in him all things were created, in heaven and on earth, visible and invisible, whether thrones or dominions or principalities or authorities; all things were created through him and for him."

What more could be said concerning our Lord as the creative agent of the universe? In what clearer way could the facts be expressed? Whatever else one may say, it is clear that, for the writers of the New Testament and Paul in particular, Jesus Christ was preeminent in the creative processes through which the universe was framed.

He Is Preeminent in Redemption

According to the heretics at Colossae, one had to understand and appease a whole host of angelic beings before one could have salvation. Besides this, their formula for salvation included the observance of the minutiae of legalistic ceremonies. They had food laws and observed new moon festivals and sabbaths.

Against all of these things Paul lashed out as he militated against these heretics in his epistle to the church at Colossae. Hear him as he speaks of the preeminence of Christ in redemption:

And you who were dead in trespasses and the uncircumcision of your flesh, God made alive together with him having forgiven us all our trespasses, having canceled the bond which stood against us with its legal demands; this he set aside, nailing it to the cross. He disarmed the principalities and powers and made a public example of them, triumphing over them in it.

That is, through Christ and his cross, God has disarmed the heretic's hierarchy of angelic powers and redeemed his people from their sins.

It is still true today. Redemption can be had only through Jesus Christ and his sacrifice. Because of what he did, we can experience salvation and come to God through the forgiveness of our sins. This cannot be experienced through any other means or person. Jesus Christ is preeminent in redemption.

He Is Preeminent in the Church

For the heretics, Christ was not the Lord of the church. They assigned him a place in the hierarchy, but he was not preeminent. For Paul, there could be no middle ground. Note his statement: "He is the head of the body, the church." If Christ is not the Lord of the church, then the church is not true to its calling. The lordship of Christ in his church is one of the more important, if not the most important, Christian doctrine. We speak of Christ as Lord, but too often it is mere lip service. Our relationship to Christ through the church is significant. The church belongs to Christ and we belong to him through his church. We do not come to Christ through the church, but we come into the church through Christ. Christ is the door to the church! The church is not the door to Christ! When a person comes to Christ, he is a part of the church whether or not he knows it or accepts it. You cannot have one without the other. When a person says: "I love Jesus but I'll have nothing to do with the church," his theology is awry. Christ loved the church and gave himself for it. It is his bride, his first love, and he will not forsake it. Now if the church belongs to Christ and we to him through his church, why do we so often act as though the church belonged to us? We speak of the autonomy of the church, and that is well and good. However, if we are to be true to Scripture, the church is autonomous only under the lordship of Christ. Whatever the church does, it should do it with this in mind. The church is to be a true theocracy with Christ as its head. We are the body and Christ is the head "from whom the whole body, nourished and knit together through its joints and ligaments, grows with a growth that is from God." In other words, it is from God through Christ that we receive our spiritual sustenance.

In all of the church's programs, Christ should be preeminent. Too often in our hustle and bustle we make the program preeminent rather than seeing it as a means to the end of making Christ preeminent. Now I believe that to properly function a church must be organized. For this to occur, it is inevitable that there be programs, goals, and slogans. My plea is that these tools be kept in proper perspective as we seek to magnify Christ through them. Any program that does not magnify Christ has no place in his church.

He Is Preeminent in the Christian's Life

That Christ is preeminent in creation and redemption cannot be denied nor can the facts be altered. These are objective facts. When it comes to giving him preeminence on our own individual lives, it is a very different matter. This is a subjective proposition. As you and I well know, Christ is not preeminent in the lives of far too many who name the name of Christ.

Paul alerts his readers to this problem in chapter 3 of Colossians. Hear him in verse 1: "If then you have been raised with Christ, keep on seeking the things that are above, where Christ is, seated at the right hand of God."

What does it mean for Christ to be preeminent in our lives? It means to give him first place in the decision-making processes. It means to allow him to direct us in our daily walk. It means doing certain things and refraining from doing others. It means to seek his face daily in prayer and Bible study. It means to give our employer a fair days work for our wages. It means for husbands and wives to be faithful to each other in all things. It means for children to obey their parents and show them proper respect. It means, in Paul's words, to "put on then as God's chosen ones, holy and beloved, compassion, kindness, lowliness, meekness, and patience . . . and above all these put on love which is the bond of maturity. And let the peace of Christ rule in your hearts."

8

The One Through Whom God Speaks

In many parts and in many ways God spoke to the fathers in times past in the prophets, but in the last of these days he spoke to us by a Son, whom he appointed heir of all things, through whom also he made the worlds. Who being the radiance of his glory and the express image of his substance, hearing about all things by the word of his power; after he made purification for sins, he sat down on the right hand of the majesty on high (Heb. 1:1-3).

The writer of the letter to the Hebrews presents Christ as one who is superior to all of the Old Testament revelation. He affirms that it is through Christ that God has spoken ultimately and finally to mankind. There is no doubt in the writer's mind that God has spoken in times past. God spoke in "many portions and in many ways" (Heb. 1:1, NASB). The writer emphasized the fact that God spoke in times past to his people through the prophets. Probably this is a reference to the entire Old Testament revelation. As the prophets delivered God's message, it was in "many portions and in many ways."

From time to time the prophets had spoken, always fitting their message to the needs of their age. Their message was never static or irrelevant, but it was adapted to the needs of their generation. But at the same time their message was fragmentary. It is interesting to note that generally a prophet's message was characterized by one central theme or idea. The message of Amos was a cry for social justice. Isaiah grasped the holiness of God as few ever have. Hosea realized and proclaimed the wonderful forgiving love of God.

The prophets also used many methods to impart God's revelation to their generations. They spoke their message and they wrote it as well. When these failed, they dramatized God's message by their actions.

Once, when Jeremiah was trying to impress the people of Judah concerning the impending judgment of God upon them, he placed a wooden yoke about his neck and walked through the streets of Jerusalem. He told the people of Judah that God would use the Babylonians to place the yoke of bondage upon them. When the official priests of Judah heard him, they wrestled the yoke from Jeremiah and broke it. Then they contradicted Jeremiah's message saying that God would break the Babylonians as they had broken the yoke of wood. Jeremiah found a yoke of iron and came back. He proclaimed the same message, and he said in effect, "Now see if you can break this yoke." The revelation of the prophets was great and manifold, but it was fragmentary in many parts and many ways.

Now the writer tells us that God has spoken to us through his Son. This is not a fragmentary revelation, but it is the ultimate revelation of God. The prophets grasped a part of the mind of God; Jesus is the very mind of God. The prophets spoke truly the word of God; Jesus is God's Word incarnate. The prophets spoke the truth about God; Jesus is God in truth. The message of the prophets was partial; Jesus is God's final word to men. This in no way depreciates the work of the prophets for they were true spokesmen for God, but Jesus is God in the flesh.

The importance of this full and final revelation of God can be seen by what this passage tells us about Jesus. This is one of the loftiest statements concerning the person and work of our Savior to be found in all of the New Testament. Notice the marvelous characterization which the writer gives of our Lord in verses 2-4 of this passage.

First he affirms that God appointed him "heir of all things." This characterization has to do with his mediatorial office. As the heir, he opens to us the way to God. The future belongs to him as the heir of all things. This is a promise that evil will not ultimately triumph. It may appear that the devil is holding sway, but Christ dealt the decisive blow to the devil and the forces of evil at the cross and the empty tomb.

During World War II, a decisive battle was fought on the European front that turned the tide of the war in favor of the Allied forces. This was referred to as D day. From that day forward it was simply a matter of time before the Allies concluded the war in Europe. The final battle was referred to as V-day because the ultimate victory belonged to the Allied forces. However, the turning point in the struggle was D day. D day for the Christian is found in the cross and resurrection of our Lord. Though V-day is still in the future, it has been assured because of what our Lord has already accomplished for us. He is the heir of all things.

Our writer also states that the worlds were created through him. This indicates that, in his preincarnate state, our Lord was the active agent in the creation of the universe. When the worlds were framed, it was the eternal Christ who exercised the power of the creative fiat of the eternal sovereign of the universe.

The writer of this beautiful letter also affirms that the original glory of God belongs to Jesus. As sunshine is of the sun and light is the expression of light, so Jesus is the radiance of God. When we look at him, we see the true expression of the character of God. We cannot see the Father's glory except in Christ. A five-year-old girl was busy marking on a piece of paper, and her mother asked: "Honey, what are you doing?" The child replied, "I'm drawing a picture of God." "But, honey," her mother replied, "no one knows what God looks like." "They will when I get through," answered the child. We may not know what God looks like, but we know what he *is* like. For Jesus is the exact representation or the reflection of his image.

In addition our writer describes Jesus as the one who "upholds all things by the word of His power." In addition to the creative word by which he brought worlds into being there is the power by which it is maintained. The phrase "the word of His power" could be rendered by our English expression "His powerful word." Christ is not pictured here as an Atlas supporting the world like a dead weight upon his shoulders. Rather he is sustaining and maintaining his creation as the one who carries all things forward on their appointed course. There is a purpose and a goal for life as well as for the whole creation, and Jesus is the one who leads us all toward that goal. Only through him can we realize our true purpose in life.

To Jesus also belongs the redemptive work. He "made purification for sins." At this point we pass from the preincarnate cosmic functions of our Lord to his incarnate work. There is a hint here of his high-priestly work which is developed throughout this letter. As we contemplate his work as creator and sustainer of the universe we may be moved to wonderment and awe. However, as we consider his activity during his incarnation and contemplate the grace which has provided the cure for the defilement produced by sin through his life freely offered upon the cross, we should be moved to such an extent that our hearts cry out in thanksgiving for the salvation which is ours in him.

To our Lord also belongs the place of mediatorial exaltation. He has taken his place at the "right hand of the Majesty on high." The tremendous thought of our writer is that our Lord is there not to judge us but to intercede for us. He is there to direct us into the presence of God. What a tremendous thought this is! The one through whom God speaks has spoken to us of God's love and concern for us. Beyond this he has invited us to come with him into the presence of the God who has spoken.

9

The True Vine

I am the true vine and my father is the farmer. Every branch in me that does not bear fruit, he removes, and everyone that bears fruit he cleanses in order that it may bear more fruit. Already you are cleansed ones because of the word which I have spoken to you. Abide in me, and I in you. Just as the branch cannot bear fruit by itself unless it should abide in the vine, thus neither can you, unless you abide in me. I am the vine and you are the branches. The one who abides in me and I in him the same shall bear much fruit, because apart from me you can do nothing. If anyone should not abide in me, he is cast away as a branch and withers, and they gather these and cast them into a fire and they are burned. If you abide in me and my word abide in you, ask what you will and it shall be done for you. In this is my Father glorified, that you should bear much fruit and be my disciples (John 15:1-8).

In John 15:1 Jesus referred to himself as the true vine. To his disciples this figure of speech had a great deal of meaning, but we may wonder just what Jesus had in mind when he chose this kind of picture language to refer to himself.

The vine certainly was not a noble tree when compared to the oak or the cedar. It was cultivated for its fruit, but its wood could not be used in the building trades. When it was cut, it was scarcely fit for anything but burning. In Ezekiel 15:1-5 we find God speaking to the prophet concerning the vine.

Then the word of the Lord came to me saying, "Son of man, how is the wood of the vine better than any wood of a branch which is among the trees of the forest? Can wood be taken from it to make anything, or can men take a peg from it on which to hang any vessel? If it has been put in the fire for fuel, and the fire has consumed both of its ends, and its middle part has been charred, is it then useful for anything? Behold, while it is intact, it is not made into anything. How much less, when the fire has consumed it and it is charred, can it still be made into anything! (NASB).

Throughout the prophetic literature of the Old Testament, the vine is used as a symbol of Israel. However, it is never used in a complimentary sense. Always it is used to characterize the degenerate state of God's people. In Ezekiel 15:6 we read: "Therefore, thus says the Lord God, 'As the wood of the vine among the trees of the forest, which I have given to the fire for fuel, so have I given up the inhabitants of Jerusalem'" (NASB). Then in Jeremiah 2:21 we find this: "Yet I planted you a choice vine,/A completely faithful seed. How then have you turned yourself before Me/Into the degenerate shoots of a foreign vine?" (NASB). Then, of course, the familiar parable of Isaiah 5:1-7 in which the poignant plight of a degenerate people is lamented. The vineyard was planted on a fertile hill and was tended with all of the care which vinedressers could lavish upon it. Yet it produced wild or worthless grapes. The explanation of the parable is given in verse 7: "For the vineyard of the Lord of hosts is the house of Israel,/And the men of Judah His delightful plant./Thus He looked for justice, but behold, bloodshed;/For righteousness, but behold, a cry of distress" (NASB).

From these references it can be seen that Israel was God's chosen vine, but they had not fulfilled the purpose for which God had chosen them. They had grown up wild and degenerate. They were worthless to their God, and because of this they faced judgment.

There is one thing that should be noted about the vine. Though its wood was worthless, it could be pruned down to the stump and still grow back to produce fruit. In fact, for the vine to be as fruitful as it should it must be pruned almost mercilessly. Thus Israel was always able to survive the onslaught of history and the severe judgment of God to sprout forth again and ultimately to bring forth the promised Messiah. Cut down a cedar tree to its stump and it is finished. Cut the vine back to its stump and it will grow again. In fact the vine is almost indestructible.

This, then, is something of the historical background of the imagery of the vine as the symbol of Israel. What can we say of the immediate circumstances that called forth Jesus' use of this imagery of himself? When Jesus taught in this fashion, there usually were physical elements in his immediate surroundings that suggested the use of the imagery. In John 6, after feeding the multitudes, Jesus gave the bread of life discourse. In John 4, the woman at the well called forth the discourse about living water. Surely there was something in their surroundings that called forth this discourse on the true vine. Several suggestions have been made by commentators through the years as to the physical surroundings that might have called forth this analogy. Perhaps there was a vineyard near to the place where the farewell supper was held. Another suggestion is that there were surely vineyards on the slopes of the Mount of Olives, and the party would have passed through them on their way to Gethsemane. In his "Antiquities of the Jews" (XV.XI. 3), Josephus describes the vine made of gold that was inlaid on the great doors of the Temple in Jerusalem. He says: "under the crown-work, was spread out a golden vine, with its branches hanging down from a great height, the largeness and fine workmanship of which were a surprising sight to the spectators." As Jesus and his disciples were going from the upper room to the Mount of Olives, they had to pass through the Temple area. The beautiful sight of the golden vine may have suggested this analogy to Jesus. As they moved out of the city toward their goal, they had to pass the valley where the refuse of Jerusalem smoldered in a continual fire. This could have suggested the imagery of judgment which also is a part of the discourse.

What then did Jesus mean when he said: "I AM the true vine"? In the first place, Jesus intended to emphasize the fact that he and he alone is the true vine. The *New American Standard Bible* translators preserved this nuance about as well as it can be preserved in English by the use of all capital letters in "I AM." Jesus wanted his disciples to understand this clearly for his death was close at hand, and he knew the trauma that the events surrounding his death would hold for them.

The word translated "true" here connotes the idea of real or genuine. He wanted them to know that he was not the shadow of the reality; he was the reality itself. The language of the statement indicates that our Lord was identifying this image with himself and was saying that he was the genuine fulfilment of the imagery represented here.

That the vine was representative of Israel is a fact of history. On the coins of the Maccabean era, Israel was represented as a vine. In the Old Testament and intertestamental literature the vine is used as a symbol of Israel. The golden inlaid vine on the great doors of the Temple of which Josephus wrote further corroborates the imagery. Jesus was saying to his disciples: "What Israel was in a figure I am in reality."

When Jesus made this assertion, he also involved the Father in the relationship. The words "My Father is the vinedresser" indicate the closeness of the relationship between the work of our Lord and his heavenly Father. It was the master plan of heaven that he was fulfilling while on the earth in his flesh. His work was one ordained of God, and in his person he fulfilled the purpose of Israel and called out a new people of God. He was saying "I am the Messiah, and the true destiny of Israel is fulfilled in who I am and in the work I have come to do." Beyond this, he spoke of his disciples as the branches.

By the use of this figure of speech, he was telling them that his messianic work included the forming of the new people of God or the new Israel of God.

There can be no productivity for the branches apart from the vine, said Jesus. Earlier it was noted that the wood of the vine was worthless as far as the building trades were concerned. The only way the branches of a vine were worth anything at all was through the fruit which they bore, and no fruit could be produced unless there was an organic connection to the stump of the vine.

By following this analogy we can understand that what Jesus had in mind throughout this discourse was the comparative usefulness or uselessness of his people. He was calling out a new people of God, so that, through him, they might fulfill the purposes of God as the new Israel. However, this goal can be accomplished only to the extent that God's people are organically connected to the source of their life and sustenance which is Jesus Christ. Just as there can be no life or sustenance for the branches of the vine unless there is that connection to the vine itself, so there can be no life or sustenance for the church apart from the true vine. As the branch of the vine can produce no fruit apart from its union with the vine, so there can be no fruit produced by God's people apart from their union with Christ who is the true vine. Without that vital union with him our purpose for being is frustrated. Paul's analogy of Christ as the head and the church as his body contains the same message for believers as does Jesus' imagery concerning himself as the vine and his followers as the branches (Eph. 4:15-16; Col. 2:19).

In the imagery of the true vine there is one further lesson for Christians. If there is life and sustenance, there is also judgment. Even at the time of the discourse, judgment was already at work in their midst. A dead branch that was attached to the vine had been pruned and was facing the fire of judgment. This dead vine was Judas. There was no life in him because he had never known a vital organic union with the true vine. This should be a warning to every person who seeks to connect themselves to the church without a vital union with Christ.

Beyond the fiery judgment which awaits those who have not been united to the true vine, there is the cleansing and pruning judgment that is continually at work in the lives of those fruit-bearing branches. As this work of pruning is done, the capacity for fruit-bearing increases. When we feel the loving hands of the Master Gardener at work pruning the branches of our life, we should rejoice because we are being prepared for bearing more fruit.

Every year scores of young people enroll in one of our six Southern Baptist seminaries for the purpose of preparing themselves for the ministry to which the Lord has called them. Some of them have already been successful in occupations for which they had prepared themselves. They have thought that the thrust of their lives would be in fields other than those generally thought of as professional ministry. The plans for their lives changed suddenly when the Master Gardener began his work of pruning in their lives. Because of this, they leave a rewarding and well-paying position to enroll in one of our seminaries to prepare for an altogether different thrust for their lives.

As branches attached to the true vine, we can bear fruit effectively only as we allow our Lord to prune and cleanse us as he gives direction to our lives.

10
Savior

And there were shepherds in this same territory staying out by night with their sheep keeping watch over them. And an angel of the Lord stood before them and the glory of the Lord shined around them, and they feared with a great fear. And the angel said to them: "Stop being afraid, for behold I bring to you good news and great joy which shall be to all people; because to you this day was born in the city of David a Savior who is Christ the Lord (Luke 2:8-11).

"Savior Like a Shepherd Lead Us"; "A Wonderful Savior"; "Jesus, Savior, Pilot Me" are just a few of the Christian hymns which extol Jesus as Savior. Indeed, in twentieth-century Christianity, Savior is one of the chief titles for Jesus, as it has been since the second Christian century. However, in the New Testament and particularly in the Gospels there are few references to Jesus by the title Savior. Also there is no record that Jesus ever used this title of himself.

The title was used of God sparingly in the Old Testament, but it was not used at all of the hoped-for Messiah. In fact, the title is not used for Messiah in the intertestamental literature, in the writings of the Dead Sea community, or in rabbinic literature. This is so probably because the title was popularly used of the kings of Egypt, Greece, Rome, and Syria. The title was also used of great men such as successful generals or important governmental officials. To put it in another way, the title in this era of history was more mundane than divine. Any great man who was involved in bringing deliverance of any sort was known as savior.

Jesus—Savior

Recorded in Matthew 1:21 is the statement of the angel to Joseph: "You shall call his name Jesus, for it is he who will save his people from their sins." In ancient Israel a man's name was supposed to be a clue to his character. If his name did not match his character, he was given a nickname that did. James and John were called "sons of thunder" because of their quick tempers. Jesus changed Simon's name to Peter because he had a rock-like character. The Greek name Jesus is the same as the Hebrew name Joshua which means salvation is of the Lord. Thus, by indicating to Joseph that he was to name the child Jesus, the angel was designating him as Savior. His function was made explicit. "It is he who will save his people from their sins."

This fact well may be a clue as to why the earliest Christians did not refer to Jesus as Savior. His name for them was indicative of his function as savior. For an Aramaic-speaking Christian the combination Jesus Savior would have been like saying Jesus-Jesus or Savior-Savior. In other words a redundancy was involved.

By AD 70 Christianity was rapidly becoming a Gentile movement and most Christians spoke Greek. Therefore they had little if any understanding of Aramaic or Hebrew. For them there was no problem or redundancy involved in saying Jesus Savior just as there is none for the twentieth-century Christian.

The Function

Though the title Savior is not found often in the Gospels, the function is apparent throughout the gospel record. The angel's message to Joseph recorded in Matthew 1:21 and the angelic chorus recorded in Luke 2:11 laid the foundation for the saving work of our Lord.

In Mark 10:45 and Matthew 20:28 his saving function is described in terms of giving his life as "a ransom for many." The word "ransom" carries the idea of an instrument or means used in setting one free from something. Perhaps this was from slavery, imprisonment, or indebtedness, but always there was a cost involved in the setting free. Jesus said that his life given was the cost involved in setting men free from sin. The words of "Jesus Paid It All" express the essence of the theology found in the ransom saying. Though the saying has no organic connection with the word *savior,* it has everything to do with our Lord's function as Savior.

Jesus said in John 10:11 "I am the good shepherd. The good shepherd lays down his life for the sheep." Here the emphasis is on our Lord's identity as the shepherd for the "I am" is quite emphatic. It is as though Jesus was saying I and no other. Though the function was not primary to his affirmation, it certainly was an integral part of it. As the good shepherd, he willingly gave his life for his sheep. There surely are echoes here of his function as Savior, for it was through this willing giving of his life that his work as Savior was accomplished.

There are at least four stages or phases to our Lord's work as Savior present in the New Testament. Though there certainly should not be any sharp demarcation in these as far as function is concerned, these stages are still visible.

In the first place he has come to man from God to be the Savior of the world. In 1 John 4:14 we read: "And we have beheld and bear witness that the Father has sent the Son *to be* the savior of the world." That is to say the origin of his work as Savior is to be found in the heart of God. The essence of this idea is found beautifully and meaningfully expressed in the words of John 3:16. One of the grandest themes of tongue or pen is the fact that God sent his Son to be the Savior of the world.

Beyond that it can be affirmed that the New Testament bears witness to the fact that our Lord's saving work was done as a man on the plane of history. His function as Savior was first shared with Joseph when the angel told Joseph what his name should be. That Jesus was aware of his saviorhood can be seen throughout his earthly ministry. The fact that much of his time on earth was spent healing the sick, cleansing lepers, and giving sight to the blind surely is an indication that he interpreted his function to be that of Savior. Though these activities have to do with the physical and spiritual well-being of those affected, there is surely a correlation to be seen between physical and spiritual well-being.

When Jesus gave sight to the man born blind (John 9), he moved quickly from the realm of the physical to that of the spiritual. In John 9:39 we find these words: "And Jesus said: 'For judgment I came into this world, so that those who do not see should see and those who see should become blind.'" On occasion Jesus connected physical healing with the forgiveness of sin (Matt. 9:1-8). As Jesus ministered to those with whom he came into contact, his interest was focused upon the whole person. Thus his function as Savior surely has to do with every aspect of human life.

The ransom saying of Mark 10:45 points to his role as Savior even though the title is not to be found in the passage. The idea of salvation is quite prominent in the ransom motif. The word *ransom* basically means to set free and this is very close to the meaning of the word for save.

Though the statement is negative, the derogatory statement of those standing by the cross has relevance for his function as Savior. In Mark 15:31 the chief priests and others mocked him by saying: "He saved others; He cannot save himself." Though they viewed the act through which salvation was obtained, their eyes were blinded to the significance of it. Surely the work of salvation was wrought out in the plane of history.

In the earliest Christian affirmation of the saviorhood of our Lord there is a note of exaltation. Acts 5 records the account of how the apostles were arrested by the Temple authorities because of their testimony and placed in a public jail. Miraculously they were released and instructed by the angel to "go your way, stand and speak to the people in the temple the whole message of this life" (v. 20). While they were following the angel's orders, the authorities apprehended them and issued them a stern rebuke and warning. In the face of this warning Peter made this statement concerning Jesus: "He is the one whom God exalted to His right hand as a Prince and a Savior, to grant repentance to Israel and forgiveness of sins" (Acts 5:31, NASB). As a result of his saving work, our Lord was exalted to the right hand of the Father as Savior.

Finally, the New Testament knows a phase of our Lord's work as Savior that we may call futuristic. Twice in Paul's letters he made reference to the saviorhood of Christ in relation to the second coming.

In Philippians 3:20 Paul said to his readers: "For our citizenship is in heaven, from which also we eagerly wait for a Savior, the Lord Jesus Christ" (NASB). In Titus 2:13 he wrote: "Looking for the blessed hope and the appearing of the glory of our great God and Savior, Christ Jesus" (NASB). These statements certainly do not indicate that Paul viewed Christ's work as Savior to be limited to his second coming, but they surely can be construed to mean that Paul saw in the event of the second coming the ultimate completion of our Lord's work as Savior.

What does it mean to us as Christians that Christ is our Savior? Our constant usage of the term may have made it seem almost common to us. We ought never to let our spiritual sensitivities become so dulled that the beauty and majesty of this title for our Lord escape our conscious comprehension. In the work that our Lord did as Savior there is a world of beautiful meaning. The ideas of release are all found in the New Testament uses of the verb to save. As Savior, Jesus has released us from the bondage of sin, rescued us from the danger of eternal judgment, preserved us for heaven, and healed the wounds of sin in our lives. Because these things are true, we can sing:

A wonderful Savior is Jesus my Lord,
A wonderful Savior to me;
He hideth my soul in the cleft of the rock,
Where rivers of pleasure I see.

FANNIE J. CROSBY

11

The Image of God

Who is the image of the invisible God, the firstborn of all creation, because by him were created all things in the heavens, and upon the earth, things visible and things invisible, whether thrones or lordships, whether rules or authorities; all things were created through him and for him, and he is before all things and in him all things hold together (Col. 1:15-17).

The Greek word used here for image connotes three basic ideas: (1) to be similar, (2) to be like, and (3) to appear. The concept of image in this word can have several different shades of meaning. The word was used most frequently in classical Greek to describe an artistic representation of an object. The reproduction of an object on a flat canvas by an artist was referred to as an image. The statue of an object or person fashioned by a sculptor was spoken of as an image. The impress of a likeness on a coin also was called an image.

In the natural sense, the word was used to describe a reflection in a pool of water or in a mirror as well as an apparition. Metaphorically it was used to describe a mental image or a similitude. Often the word described an exact copy of something, a living image or likeness, as well as the embodiment of a person or a concept. The legal description of a person in a contract or a criminal on a "wanted" poster was called an image. This usage consisted of a summary of personal character traits as well as distinguishing physical marks.

Philo of Alexandria, the Jewish philosopher who sought to harmonize Old Testament Scripture with Greek philosophy spoke of the *logos* as the image of God. In the Wisdom of Solomon (a Jewish intertestamental work) wisdom is said to be the image of the goodness of God.

In the Septuagint (the Greek Old Testament) the word *image* is used thirty-six times. In Genesis 1:26 God said: "Let us make man in our image." In other words man was to bear the stamp of God upon his personality. Sixteen of these thirty-six times that the word occurs in the Septuagint it is found in Daniel's visions and to the image that King Nebuchadnezzer made of himself for his subjects to worship. Except for the several occurrences in Genesis where the word describes man as being created in the image of God, the word always has reference to some physical image. Generally these images are in the form of idols. Therefore one is safe in concluding that the philosophical use of the word is nonexistent in the Old Testament with the notable exception of the early chapters of Genesis.

In the New Testament the word is found twenty-two times with a variety of uses. None of these occurrences are in Revelation where it consistently has to do with a physical representation such as an idol. In the parallel passage of Mark 12:16, Matthew 22:20, and Luke 20:24 we find the record of the question Jesus asked his detractors concerning the tribute money. "Whose is the image and the author superscription?" In other words, whose likeness is on the coin?

Paul used the word nine times in four of his letters. He used it twice in Romans, 2 Corinthians, and Colossians. In 1 Corinthians he used it three times.

In Romans 1:23 Paul was writing about Gentile man's idolatrous activities. He said that man had exchanged the glory of the incorruptible God for an image in the form of man, birds, four-footed animals, and crawling creatures. Image here is used of concrete manifestations in the form of idols.

In Romans 8:29 Paul said that redeemed humanity was predestined to the image of God's Son. Paul's use of the word *image* here is much more philosophical and intangible than was his usage in

Romans 1:23. Again in 1 Corinthians 11:7 and 15:49 he used the word in this philosophical sense. In 1 Corinthians 11:7 he spoke of man as the glory and image of God and in 15:49 he said that as mankind has borne the image of the first Adam so redeemed humanity should bear the image of the second Adam who is Christ. In 2 Corinthians 3:18 and 4:4 Paul used the word philosophically for man being changed to the image of Christ and Christ being the image of God. In Colossians 3:10 he used the word to describe the likeness of the new man in Christ to the one who created him.

In Hebrews 10:1 the word *image* is used in a way that is different from every other New Testament usage. The writer spoke of the law as a "shadow of the good things to come *and* not the very image of things." Some English translations use the word *form* to translate image. The idea in the word here is that of reality as opposed to shadow.

With the exception of Romans 1:23 the only New Testament document that uses image to refer to concrete images used for the purposes of idolatry is Revelation. For Paul, who used the word in more different ways than any other New Testament writer, the idea in image was primarily philosophical.

In Colossians 1:15 he described Christ as the "image of the invisible God." To modern logic this is a contradiction. How can there be an image of that which is without form? Surely, then, we can eliminate the meaning of image that has to do with a concrete likeness. The word here is related to that usage which is not limited to a functional representation that is received by our human senses of sight or touch. The word does not here imply a feeble copy of something. Rather it implies the illumination of its inner core and essence. To put it another way, image represents the reality itself. When we see Christ, we see God. We do not see all there is of God, but everything that we see in Christ is the image of God. In John 14:8-9 it is recorded that Philip asked Jesus to show them the Father, and Jesus replied: "He who has seen me has seen the Father"

(NASB). Jesus did not mean to say that he exhausted the person of the Godhead, but he did claim to be a perfect manifestation and representation of God in his person. This is the idea Paul was expressing by his statement in Colossians 1:15. A group of false teachers in Colossae had sought to rob Christ of his rightful place in the Godhead, and Paul was writing to correct this problem.

Paul made four assertions concerning Christ as the image of God. (1) He is the firstborn of all creation; (2) He created all things; (3) He is before all things; and (4) All things have their existence in him. These are pointed statements concerning the person of our Lord. They seem to assert that what Jesus did is based on who he is. Though two of these assertions are basically functional, they still have primary reference to who Jesus is.

When Paul said that Jesus was the firstborn of all creation, he was not by any stretch of the imagination saying that he was a created being. This is made explicit in the next statement. Normally the word has to do with natural birth, but the only time in the New Testament that is used this way of Jesus is in Luke 2:7 where it is said of Mary that "she brought forth her firstborn son." Everywhere else that it is used of Jesus it has the meaning of the first principle. Some have suggested that the word should be given a hierarchical meaning here. The first-born son among Jews received many privileges which others did not share. Paul used the term of Jesus in this way in Romans 8:29 where he spoke of Jesus as the "first-born among many brethren." It seems that in Colossians 1:15 Paul was thinking rather of the importance of our Lord in his preexistent state to the overall creative process. Paul was not affirming that Jesus came into being prior to all of the rest of creation but that he is the one through whom all of creation came into being.

In verse 16 Paul made a comprehensive statement concerning the role of Christ in his preexistent state as the creative agent through whom all created things came into being. Things in the heavens and upon the earth were brought into being by his creative power. By this all-encompassing statement Paul was thinking about the natural universe. The earth and all that is in it as well as the starry heavens which have always held such a mystery for all mankind were included. Things which are visible and things which are invisible also were within the area of his creative fiat. Whether they were a part of the natural order of things as we behold it or whether they were beyond our understanding, Paul wanted his readers to know that our Lord's creative activity was all inclusive. Thrones, lordship, rules, and authorities in all likelihood were used in reference to a hierarchy of angelic powers. Perhaps this was the hierarchy that was envoked by the false teachers at Colossae. The first order called thrones occurs in the intertestamental work the Testament of Levi. There they are placed in the seventh heaven, and presumably they were heavenly beings that occupied thrones around the throne of God. They are not mentioned elsewhere in the New Testament. When the other words are found in sequence in the New Testament, the reference is generally to supernatural powers, but they are always subject to God in Christ. That is so by virtue of the fact that they have come into being as a result of his creative activity.

As though his first assertion were not sufficient, Paul repeated his statement that Christ was responsible for creating all of these. In the first instance Paul used a tense of the verb "create" which viewed his creative work as a single act. In this last usage he employed a tense which views the creative work from the perspective of a completed process. Each time he used the same verb which basically means to bring order out of confusion.

Paul's next assertion is that Christ is before all things. The idea here is more than just the fact that he existed prior to all things, though this is the predominant idea. Surely we must affirm with the writers of the New Testament that our Lord is eternal. He knew no beginning and shall know no end. His existence is prior to all things and is not predicated on anything or anyone. As he said to the Pharisees: "Before Abraham was I am" (John 8:58). As the creator of all things, he surely is also superior to all. Though this construction does not necessarily contain this idea, the context surely allows this intimation. Therefore our Lord exists prior to all creation and he is superior to all creation.

The final ssertion that Paul made concerning our Lord as the image of God is that in him all things hold together or have their existence. The word here can have five possible meanings in the New Testament. In the form that the word appears here the idea is to have their existence or possibly to maintain their coherence. He is the bond of all things, the one who holds them together indissolubly and binds them fast. From the smallest atom in the microcosm to the largest galaxy in the macrocosm he gives coherence and maintains order. This is a most inclusive statement concerning our Lord's relation to the created universe. He is not only the creative agent of the Sovereign God, but he is the sustainer of the universe.

Thus, by using the term the image of God, Paul was setting forth his estimation of the person of our Lord. It was his conviction that Jesus was not merely a dim reflection of God, but in him the reality of God can be seen. To use a term prevalent in the Jewish vocabulary of Paul's day, in Jesus we see the *Shekinah* present in human form. God is invisible so we cannot see him, but he has sent his Son to us in visible form. By looking at him we can see the exact representation in human form of the invisible God. To the question, What is God like? Paul would have said: "Look at Jesus and you will know exactly what God is like."

12

Lord

Therefore, let all of the house of Israel know assuredly that God made him both Lord and Christ, this Jesus whom you crucified (Acts 2:36).

And he has upon his garment and upon his thigh a name written: King of kings and Lord of lords (Rev. 19:16).

The Background

Since the very early days of the Christian church, one of the most exalted titles for Jesus Christ has been that of Lord. In fact it seems that quite early this title came to be used almost as a part of his name. Of course, Jesus is his given name; Christ is a title which means Anointed One or Messiah; and Lord is a title of exaltation.

There has been much debate and speculation among New Testament scholarship concerning the reason for the use of this title for Jesus by the early church. There is little doubt that this word was in wide usage in the Greco-Roman world of the first century. Yet, in spite of the fact of its almost universal usage in a variety of ways in the Greek-speaking world of the first century it became for Christians a title that was to be used only for the Lord of the church, Jesus Christ. How did this happen? What caused the early Christians to zero in on such a common title as this and conclude that it was to be used exclusively for Jesus Christ?

Any good dictionary of the Greek language will inform us that the word *lord (kurios)* means owner, master, or lord. Beyond this the word had a variety of usages in the first century. It was used quite often in polite address in the way that our English words *sir* or *madam* might be used. In John 12:20-21 we find the record of the Greeks coming to Philip asking him to take them to Jesus. In so doing they addressed Philip as "lord," though the English translations generally render it as "sir." The second letter of John is addressed to the "elect lady" according to our English translations, but literally the Greek is the *elect kuria.* Now *kuria* is the feminine form for lord, which was the polite form of address for a respected lady.

A student would have addressed his teacher as lord. This quite often is the import of the title when applied to Jesus in the Gospels, particularly when we find the word on the lips of one of the apostles. In very few instances is the word used of Jesus in the Gospels with overtones of exaltation that was later given to the term by the early Christians. In Luke 24:3 it is said that on the first day of the week the women came to the tomb but they did not find the body of the "Lord Jesus." In John 20:2 Mary Magadlene told Simon and the other disciple whom Jesus loved: "They have taken away the Lord." In Luke 2:11 we find that the angel spoke to the shepherds of the birth of a "Savior, who is Christ the Lord." Generally, however, the title as used of Jesus in the Gospels is an address of respect but not a title of exaltation.

When a soldier spoke to his superior in the first century, he would have addressed him as lord much in the same way that a soldier addresses an officer as sir today. When a Roman official addressed the emperor or spoke of the emperor, he used the title Lord. In Acts 25:25-26 we find recorded the statement of Festus to Agrippa concerning Paul. Speaking of the emperor he called him "my lord."

The word would have been used by a slave when addressing his master. It was used of landowners. For instance in Mark 12:9 the landowner is called the lord of the vineyard. Any petty government official would have been called lord by those of the citizenry who spoke to them, and they likewise would have addressed their superiors as lord.

A Greek-speaking son when addressing his father would refer to him as "Lord." In Matthew 21:29-30 we find a record of this occurring, though "lord" is sometimes translated by the English word *sir*. There also are letters preserved from the Greek world of the first century where a son referred to his father as lord.

In the mystery religions of the first century the title "lord" was used to refer to the deity of a particular cult. In letters that have been preserved from the Greek world of the first-century deities were often invoked to bless the one to whom the letter was being sent. For instance, the sender might say: "I have prayed to the lord Serapis that you will prosper and be preserved in health."

Perhaps the most insidious usage as far as Christians were concerned in the first century was that within the cult of the Roman emperors. Generally, when a Roman emperor died, he was elevated to the state of a god. However, certain people wished to proclaim the deity of the living emperors. Nero (54-68) and some of those who came after him (notably Domitian and Trajan) took seriously the idea that they were divine. By the eighth decade of the first century emperor worship became a test of loyalty to the government of Rome. Once each year every person in the Roman Empire was required to burn a pinch of incense to Caesar and confess that "Caesar is Lord." When this was done, the person was given a certificate that he had worshiped before the shrine of the emperor, and he was free to carry on his normal life for another year. By this time, however, the title "lord" had become a fixed designation for Jesus among Christians, and they steadfastly refused to confess Caesar as lord. For this refusal many Christians were required to forfeit their lives.

The historian of the early church Eusebius Pamphilus in his work *Ecclesiastical History* tells of a martyr of the early church named Polycarp who was the bishop of the church at Smyrna. Though he was martyred in the mid second century, his experience is similar to those who in the first century were called upon to die as a testimony to the lordship of Christ in their lives. According to Eusebius, government persecution of Christians had taken the lives of certain Christians in Smyrna. The authorities were persuaded that if they captured Polycarp, the leader of the Christians in this area, and made an example of him that this might discourage others to convert to Christianity. On the advice of friends Polycarp hid himself from the authorities on a farm not far from the city. After some difficulties the authorities discovered his hiding place and took Polycarp captive.

According to Eusebius, Polycarp was cheerful and set food before his captors asking only that they provide him with one hour for uninterrupted prayer before taking him to the city. Now Polycarp was eighty-six years old, and his captors were amazed that so venerable and pious a man should be worthy of death. When the authorities were able to examine Polycarp, they asked him: "For what harm is there in saying Lord Caesar, and to sacrifice, and thus save your life?" He would not answer them at first, but when they continued he said: "I shall not do what you advise me." When they saw that they were unable to persuade him, they treated him harshly and took him to the stadium. When the proconsul saw that he was an old man, he said: "Have regard for your age and swear by the genius of Caesar." Polycarp refused, and the proconsul continued to urge him and said: "Swear and I will dismiss you." "Revile Christ?" Polycarp replied, "Eighty and six years have I served him, and he never did me wrong; and how can I now blaspheme my king that has saved me?" The proconsul continued to urge him to recant. When Polycarp would not, he threatened him with wild beasts. Polycarp still would not recant, so the proconsul threatened to burn him at the stake. With this he prayed and was burned at the stake for refusing to apply the title of Lord to Caesar.

Jesus As Lord

As was mentioned earlier, the title Lord was used often of Jesus in the Gospels but only a few times with any overtones of exaltation.

The title was reserved for him in his resurrection glory. In Acts 2:36 in Peter's powerful sermon at Pentecost we find him saying: "Therefore let all the house of Israel know assuredly that God hath made him both Lord and Christ, this Jesus whom you crucified." The title is used often in the Acts of the Apostles of Jesus in combinations such as our Lord Jesus Christ. A glance at any good New Testament concordance will demonstrate just how often the title is found in this document. The title is used in several different ways, but its use as a title of exaltation for Jesus is certain.

The apostle Paul confronted the Gentile world with the gospel quite early and between the years 51-62 he wrote thirteen letters to three individuals and seven church groups. In these letters he used the title "lord" more than two hundred times to refer to Jesus. Quite often the title "lord" occurs alone in reference to Jesus. Many times it is used in combinations such as "the Lord Jesus," "the Lord Jesus Christ," "Jesus Christ our Lord," and "Christ Jesus our Lord." There can be little doubt that for Paul the title "lord" was one which carried with it the idea of exaltation when used of Jesus.

Throughout the remainder of the New Testament this title is also applied to Jesus with some frequency, and always there is the idea of exaltation contained within it. Many of the documents of our New Testament were written for predominately Gentile congregations, and for them Jesus is preeminently the Lord. No other name for Jesus was used with such frequency as was the title lord among Gentile Christians. For Gentile Christians "the Lord" is at once a reference to the historical Jesus and the exalted Christ. Perhaps the most graphic representation of this is found in Revelation 19:16 where he is extolled as "King of kings and Lord of lords."

For some time there has been a debate among New Testament scholars as to the background for the use of the title Lord as an exalted title for Jesus. Some have argued that the wide usage of the title among Gentile Christians can be traced to its widespread usage in the pagan culture of the Gentile world. They point to the fact that important persons were regularly addressed by the title lord. Already it was used as a name for divinities as its use in the cult of emperor worship and in the mystery religions proves. They maintain that in the title lord there was an element of exaltation already present that was simply transferred to Jesus. However, it should be pointed out that the earliest Christians were Jews, and they continued to cling to the Jewish Scriptures.

The early church accepted the writings of the Old Testament as their sacred Scriptures also. When Christianity moved out to confront the Gentile world with the gospel, the Greek translation of the Old Testament (the Septuagint) became the standard Christian text for the Old Testament. In this translation lord was an important title for God. One of the Ten Commandments admonished the Hebrews not to take the name of God in vain. For fear that they might do this the Israelites would not pronounce the covenant name for God. The covenant name for God was written in the text of the Hebrew Old Testament, but it was never verbalized by the Israelites. They substituted instead the Hebrew word for lord (adoniah). When the Hebrew Old Testament was translated into Greek in Egypt in 280 BC, they would not translate the covenant name for God into Greek, so they translated the Hebrew word for lord by the Greek kurios or lord. Thus, when the earliest Greek-speaking Christians read the Old Testament, they found that the title lord was applied to the covenant name for God. It well may be that this is the reason that the Greek term lord came to be accepted as a name implying divinity by the earliest Christians. Certainly by the time Christianity moved full flush into the Gentile world the name Lord was an exalted title used exclusively for Jesus Christ with overtones of deity.

The Meaning of the Confession

What does it mean to confess Jesus as Lord? This is a question that needs to be asked today, for with the passage of the centuries there is the possibility that some of the original force of the word has been lost. The name Lord is so regularly applied to our Savior that for some it has come to be accepted as a part of his name rather than a title of exaltation and sovereignty. We need to be reminded often as Christians that the title Lord has some very definite implications for us.

In the first place the name Lord implies ownership. In the parable of Jesus the lord of the vineyard was the owner of the vineyard. In the first century the lord of a slave was his owner. If Jesus is our Lord, then we belong to him in a very real sense. We should never forget this as we walk through the vale of this life. As Paul put it in 1 Corinthians 6:19-20, we are not our own because we have been bought with a price.

Beyond that the lordship of Christ implies sovereignty. If he is our Lord, we are subject and he is sovereign. The sovereign gives the orders and the subject carries out the orders. Lord has become such a common title for Christ that we have become dulled to the idea of sovereignty that is found within it. Though our vernacular term boss does not sound nearly as exalted or spiritual as the term Lord, this essentially is what the term means from this perspective. Jesus asked his followers: "Why do you call me Lord, Lord, and refuse to do the things I tell you?" If he were in the flesh today, he well might ask us as his followers this same question. It is one thing to confess him as Lord with our lips, but it is quite another matter to make him Lord of our lives in reality.

Of all the titles applied to Jesus this one implies exaltation perhaps more than any other. So exalted was their view of Jesus as Lord that the early Christians would not allow anyone else to claim the title. Even the emperor of Rome was not allowed to share this title with their exalted Lord. As Lord he was raised from the dead and seated at the right hand of God in the heavens. His place of preeminence was unquestioned and this title expressed the mind of the early church in this regard. The apostle Paul echoed this sentiment when he wrote to the Philippians that "At the name of Jesus every knee shall bow and every tongue confess that he is Lord to the glory of God the Father" (3:10-11).

13
Son of Man

And Jesus said to him, the foxes have holes and the birds of the heaven nests, but the Son of man has no place where he can lay his head (Matt. 8:20).

So then the Son of Man is Lord also of the sabbath (Mark 2:28).

For even the Son of Man did not come to be ministered to but to minister and to give his life a ransom for many (Mark 10:45).

And Jesus said: "I am, and you shall see the Son of Man sitting at the right hand of the power and coming with the clouds of heaven" (Mark 14:62).

So that you may know that the Son of Man has authority to forgive sins upon the earth he said to the paralytic, "I say to you, Arise take up your bed and go to your house" (Mark 2:10-11).

The Background

Because the Hebrew language had a scarcity of adjectives, the phrase "son of" was used often as a descriptive characterization where English would simply use an adjective. Thus the phrase "son of man" in the Old Testament generally is another way of saying man. This is particularly true of its usage in Ezekiel where it is found perhaps with more frequency than in any other Old Testament book. There the phrase is used particularly to describe the prophet Ezekiel and means little more than man. Though some scholars have seen a connection between the usage of the phrase in Ezekiel and Jesus' use of the title for himself, most today would turn to another Old Testament document for the background to Jesus' use.

In the book of Daniel the phrase is used to characterize a figure in one of Daniel's visions. In Daniel 7: 13-14 we read:

> I kept looking in the night visions,
> And behold, with the clouds of heaven
> One like a Son of Man was coming,
> And He came up to the Ancient of Days
> And was presented before Him.
> And to Him was given dominion,
> Glory and a kingdom,
> That all the peoples, nations, and men of every language
> Might serve him.
> His dominion is an everlasting dominion
> Which will not pass away;
> And His kingdom is one
> Which will not be destroyed (NASB).

Then in Daniel 7:18 we find: "But the saints of the Highest One will receive the kingdom and possess the kingdom forever, for all ages to come." And in 7:27: "Then the sovereignty, the dominion, and the greatness of *all* the kingdoms under the whole heaven will be given to the people of the saints of the Highest One. His kingdom *will be* an everlasting kingdom, and all the dominions will serve and obey Him" (NASB).

This heavenly man will receive the kingdom from the Most High and he will deliver it to the saints of the Most High. This passage was accepted by the Jews as messianic, and they looked for the coming of a strong man who would wrest the political rule from their oppressors and deliver it to the Jewish people. Thus they looked for a golden age of political as well as religious freedom during the messianic era.

There can be little doubt that Jesus saw his role as Messiah mirrored in the vision of Daniel 7, but he did not join with the Jews in their interpretation of it. When Pilate asked Jesus: "Are you the king of the Jews?" Jesus replied: "My kingdom is not of this world." (See John 18: 33-36). That Jesus saw his life and work as a fulfillment of the prophecy of Daniel 7 can be seen from his answer to the high priest recorded in Mark 14:62. The high priest had asked Jesus whether or not he was the Messiah. Jesus replied: "I am, and you shall see the Son of Man at the right hand of the power and coming with the clouds of heaven."

Among the literary documents of the Jews written during the period between the Testaments there is one which contains a great deal of information concerning the Son of man. This is the Similitudes of Enoch. In this document the Son of man is a preexistent heavenly man who shares the glory of God. He is also God's special envoy in bringing vengeance and judgment upon God's enemies. There are those who have sought a relationship between the Son of man in Enoch and Jesus' usage of the title. Though Enoch's Son of man could be considered as a messianic figure, Jesus seems to have rejected the strong man motif that is prevalent there.

Jesus As Son of Man

Jesus took the title Son of man as it is used in Daniel and expanded the concept. The prophecy in Daniel was accepted by Jesus as a part of his mission as Son of man, but there is more to Jesus' conception of himself as Son of man than is found in the vision of Daniel.

There can be little doubt that the title Son of man was Jesus' favorite self-designation. No one else ever used the title for Jesus in the Gospels. In Acts 7:56 Stephen used the title of Jesus, but this is the only instance in the New Testament where someone else used it of Jesus.

Though Jesus used the title in many contexts, there basically are four ways in which he used the title of himself. (1) He used the title when referring to his present activity or ministry. (2) He used it when speaking of his suffering and resurrection. (3) He employed the term when referring to his future exaltation. (4) There is evidence that within his concept of Son of man there is a reference to the redeemed community which he came to establish.

His Present Ministry

Probably the preponderance of times that Jesus used the title would be classified as relating to his present ministry as the Incarnate Messiah. These sayings pretty well run the gamut of this entire ministry.

In Luke 11:30 he said: "For just as John was a sign to the Ninevites, so shall the Son of Man be to this generation." His whole ministry was a sign to bring men to repentence just as Jonah was a sign to bring Nineveh to their knees in repentence. This saying is a reference to the impact of his entire ministry as Son of man and not to any specialized part of it.

To some who sought to follow him, Jesus reminded them that he could not offer them any physical or material security. Recorded in Matthew 8:20 is this assertion: "And Jesus said to him: 'The foxes have dens and the birds of the heaven *have* nests, but the Son of Man has no place to lay his head.' " If you are going to follow me, you must count the cost, said Jesus. There is an indication here that Jesus did not think of worldly honor and prestige as a part of his function as Son of man. He had not come to exercise brute strength to overthrow the enemies of the Jews and to set up an earthly political rule in Jerusalem. Rather he anticipated that, as Son of man, he would face hardships, and he wanted those who would be his followers to be aware of this fact.

In Mark 2:28 there is a most arresting claim of Jesus. He and his disciples had just walked through a field of standing grain on the sabbath. They had taken some of the grain, rubbed it in their hands to loosen the husks, and had blown away the husks and had eaten the grain. This infuriated the Jewish authorities for this was contrary to their oral law concerning the sabbath. Jesus and his disciples were guilty of harvesting, threshing, winnowing, and preparing a meal on the sabbath. When they accosted Jesus, he reminded them that God made the sabbath for man's benefit rather than the other way around. Then he said: "So then the Son of man is lord also of the sabbath." As the Son of man, Jesus claims to have authority over the institutions of Judaism. The fact that he made this claim in the presence of those whose responsibility it was to enforce the regulations pertaining to the sabbath has significance. Encounters such as this finally brought the wrath of the religious authorities down upon his head.

In the second chapter of Mark is found the record of four men who brought their paralytic friend to Jesus to be healed. The crowd was so great that they were not able to get their friend into the house where Jesus was. Therefore they climbed upon the roof, and they took up some of the roof sections. After they had done this, they lowered their friend through the hole in the roof. When Jesus saw their faith, he said to the paralytic: "Your sins are forgiven." This upset the authorities who were there, and they began to question among themselves concerning it. Only God can forgive sins, they reasoned. Jesus perceived their consternation and said: "Which is easier, to say to the paralytic your sins are forgiven, or to say, arise take up your bed and walk? But so that you may know that the Son of Man has authority upon the earth to forgive sins—he says to the paralytic, I say to you, arise take up your bed and go to your house." He wanted the authorities to know that he had the authority within himself as Son of man to forgive sin as well as to heal disease.

Jesus used the title Son of man when speaking of his mission upon the earth. After his interview with Zacchaeus, recorded in Luke 19:1-9, he said: "For the Son of man came to seek and to save that which was lost." His mission upon earth as Son of man was that of seeking out and saving persons like Zacchaeus who have been lost from God.

Though there are many examples like these of this usage of the title Son of man, these are representative. We have seen that, as Son of man, he would not offer material security, but he exercised authority over the sabbath as well as sin and sickness. Beyond that he spoke of his ultimate mission upon the earth in terms of his Son of man relationship.

His Suffering and Resurrection

Jesus did not use the title Messiah of himself in the first three Gospels, and he did not encourage others to use it of him. He did receive the title from Peter prior to his transfiguration and from the high priest at his trial. However, in each instance, after receiving the title, he substituted the title Son of man when making reference to himself in his reply. After Peter confessed him to be the Messiah in Mark 8:29, Jesus accepted the designation but immediately began to use the title Son of man as he spoke of his suffering and his resurrection.

Beginning at Mark 10:32 Jesus was once again speaking to his disciples of his suffering that soon was to be. In 10:33-34 he said: "Behold we are going up to Jerusalem, and the Son of Man will be delivered to the chief priests and to the scribes, and they will condemn him to death and deliver him to the Gentiles and they will mock him and spit upon him and scourge him and kill *him,* and after three days he will rise again." At the end of this statement James and John asked him to give to them the right-hand and left-hand positions by his throne when he established his rule. At this point Jesus gave them a lecture on servanthood and made one of the greatest statements ever recorded. This statement found in Mark 10:45 is a thematic statement for this Gospel. "For even the Son of Man did not come to be ministered to but to minister and to give his life a ransom for many." As Son of man, he must suffer and die as a ministry to his people. These are just representative of several contexts, but they serve to illustrate the fact that Jesus used the title Son of man in relation to his suffering and resurrection.

The majority of New Testament scholars recognize that the title Son of man was Jesus' favorite self-designation and that he used it relative to his suffering. This they say introduces the concept of the Suffering Servant into Jesus' self-interpretation. Though Jesus never spoke of himself in terms of the Suffering Servant, he did envision suffering as his chief task and he spoke of it in terms of a ministry or service. Thus he used the Son of man title and reinterpreted it, using the concept of the Suffering Servant of Isaiah. This is the chief reason why Jesus would not use the title Messiah of himself and did not encourage others to use it of him. For the Jews of the first century the title Messiah conjured up visions of a political conqueror who would overthrow the yoke of Rome and reestablish the kingdom of David in Jerusalem. This idea was so foreign to the work Jesus came to do as Messiah that he could not use the title of himself without being grossly misunderstood. Even Peter, perhaps his closest disciple, did not fully comprehend his Lord's function when he confessed him to be the Messiah (Mark 8:29). For, when Jesus began to speak of his impending suffering, Peter rebuked him. Suffering simply was not on the agenda for the Messiah as Peter understood it. Jesus faced this problem by using the title Son of man and couching it in the concept of the Suffering Servant when explaining his messianic function to his desciples.

Eschatological Exaltation

There was a time when scholars saw in the Son of man title only a solidarity with mankind. There was no element of exaltation to be found in it, they said. Their idea was that the Son of God title stressed the exalted nature of our Lord and the Son of man title his humanity and his solidarity with those he came to save. That the Son of man title does stress our Lord's humanity and his solidarity with mankind cannot be denied, but this does not exhaust the meaning of the title. Beyond this there is the evident danger that is always present when one attempts to dissect the personality of our Lord. There is the danger that he may be seen as half human and half divine rather than all human and all divine in a perfectly integrated personality. For Jesus, Son of man was the all-encompassing title for every facet of his work.

In Mark 8:38 we find a statement of Jesus that relates to his future exaltation. It is couched in a context containing a statement dealing with the cost of discipleship and it follows hard upon Peter's rebuke of Jesus. In the statement Jesus warned that if anyone were ashamed of him or his words in this sinful and adulterous generation that "the Son of man will be ashamed of him when he comes in the glory of his Father with the holy angels." There can be little doubt that the title Son of man is used as a personal reference here, even though he used the personal pronoun to refer to himself in the first half of the statement. The idea of judgment also pervades this saying of Jesus. There is no doubt that Jesus had reference to his future exaltation by this statement. This is made plain by the future tense of the verb "shall be ashamed" and by the fact he will come "in the glory of his Father with the holy angels."

Recorded in Mark 14:62 is a statement that Jesus made to the high priest during the pretrial hearing that occurred at the residence of the high priest. The false witnesses had not been able to agree among themselves concerning their accusations of Jesus. Finally in exasperation the high priest asked Jesus: "Are you the Christ the Son of the Blessed?" The word *blessed* is a circumlocution for God. Since the Jews were fearful of breaking the Third Commandment, which has to do with taking God's name in vain, they used various circumlocutions to keep from speaking God's name. The word *Christ* of course is the Greek equivalent of the Hebrew "Messiah." Jesus answered the high priest's question in the affirmative, but he changed the title Messiah to Son of man as he combined parts of Psalm 110:1 and Daniel 7:13.

Some interpreters have said that Jesus meant that the high preist and those with him would recognize that Jesus' claim was valid after the resurrection. This, however, is not borne out historically. The most obvious meaning of a statement generally is the best interpretation. Jesus appears to have cast his answer to the future, even to his second coming and the great day of judgment. At that time those who were then sitting in judgment to condemn him will know the truth of his affirmation. They will recognize the glory that belongs to him as Son of man. Thus the title Son of man belongs also to the future glory and exaltation of our Lord.

The Redeemed Community

Among the contributions to New Testament study made by the late T. W. Manson is his assertion that Jesus was not only Son of man but that he came to create the Son of man as a corporate reality in the redeemed community. This idea certainly suits the interpretation of the Daniel prophecy, and there can be little doubt that Jesus came to create a redeemed community. In Daniel 7:18 and 27 the saints of the Highest One receive the kingdom and possess it forever and ever. Though Jesus did not use the title in a fashion that undisputedly can be interpreted as communal, he did indicate that those who followed him would share in his suffering. One must be willing to "deny himself and take up his cross" (Mark 8:34). He said to James and John in Mark 10:39: "The cup which I drink you shall drink and the baptism with which I am being baptized you shall be baptized." Though he could not promise them the seats of honor, he could promise them a share of his suffering.

T. W. Manson pointed out that in the final analysis none of the disciples was willing to stand with Jesus as he created Son of man. Ultimately Jesus was crucified between two thieves rather than between two disciples, not because he refused to allow them to be crucified with him but because they did not choose to be crucified with him. Thus in creating the redeemed community he embodied in his person that perfect human response to God's sovereign claim. The redeemed community did become a reality and the rule of God has come in the lives of his followers because of what he did as Son of man.

14

The Promised Seed of Abraham

Brethren I speak as a man: Though it is only a man's covenant, after it has been ratified, no one sets it aside or adds anything to it. Now to Abraham and to his seed were the promises spoken. It does not say as to seeds, as unto many, but as unto one, and to your seed, who is Christ. Now this I say, a covenant, which has been ratified by God is not annulled by a law which came four hundred and thirty years later, so as to make the covenant of no effect. For if inheritance were of the law, it would no longer be of promise; but God granted it to Abraham by means of a promise. What then is the law? Because of transgressions it was set forth, until the seed should come to whom the promise was made, ordained through angels by the hand of a mediator (Gal. 3:15-19).

The Background

Abraham was already an old man when God called him out of Ur, and he and his wife were childless. God spoke to Abraham (who was still known as Abram Gen. 15), and told him that he would greatly reward him. Abraham protested that, since he had no child, his heir was his steward. God assured Abraham that he would give him a son. When Sarah (then called Sarai) bore no son, she gave Hagar, her handmaid, to Abraham as a wife and she bore a son who was named Ishmael. Later God promised Abraham a son from his wife Sarah. When Isaac was born, Ishmael was a teenager, and when Sarah weaned Isaac, Ishmael made light of the event. Sarah wanted Abraham to send Hagar and Ishmael away, and this distressed

Abraham. In Genesis 21:12 we read: "But God said to Abraham, 'Do not be distressed because of the lad and your maid; whatsoever Sarah tells you, listen to her, for through Isaac your descendants shall be named'" (NASB).

Jesus As the Seed of Abraham

Matthew traced the genealogy of Jesus back to Abraham and called him a son of Abraham. Luke traced Jesus' genealogy back to Adam, though in the midst of the genealogy, Abraham is mentioned as one of his progenitors. Admittedly these references are only incidental and have no bearing on Paul's argument that Jesus is the promised seed of Abraham.

Though the concept is not widely developed in the New Testament, Paul's rationale in developing it in Galatians has tremendous importance for us as Christians today. Paul hinted at his argument in Galatians 3:3-9 where he said: "Now the Scripture foreseeing that God would make the Gentiles righteous by faith preached the gospel beforehand to Abraham *saying* all the nations shall be blessed in you. So then those who are of faith are being blessed together with faithful Abraham." So then those whose lives are marked by the kind of faith that marked Abraham's life are the true heirs of the blessings of Abraham.

The major thrust of Paul's argument concerning Jesus as the promised seed of Abraham is found in Galatians 3:15-19. The primary thrust of the idea is that the promises which God made to Abraham have found fulfillment in Christ and through Christ for Christians.

In verse 15 Paul alerted his readers that he was using an analogy that had to do with human relations to enforce his point. When a human covenant or will has been ratified, no one can set it aside. This human document is not to be tampered with at all. This truth was brought home to me with a great deal of force some years ago while I was serving as pastor of the Central Baptist Church in Carthage,

Texas. Some years before I became pastor there a dear lady had established a trust fund with the church for the purpose of a student loan fund. College students whose families were members of the church there could borrow from the fund for 6 percent simple interest. At that time a lower interest rate was available from several governmental loan funds, and very few people had taken advantage of their borrowing privilege. The fund was just sitting there collecting interest. As pastor, I felt strongly that those funds should be used in some way for Christian education. I suggested to the trustees of the fund that we should make the money available to a nearby Baptist college so that the interest could be used for scholarships. The trustees thought the idea had merit but suggested we seek the counsel of the lawyer who had set up the legal matters dealing with the fund. When I approached him, he informed me in no uncertain terms that my suggestion would be a violation of the trust that had been established in the lady's will. He said that it was her desire that the fund be set up as it was and that it be used by church members. Therefore we were not free to tamper with the fund in any way.

Implied in Paul's argument is the thought that if a man's testament cannot be tampered with how much more inviolable is one that God has established. God's promises are as secure as anything that we can possibly imagine. When God makes a promise, there is nothing in this world that can invalidate that promise. This is the key point to Paul's argument in this passage.

"Now the promise" of verse 16 is a reference to those promises which God made to Abraham and to his seed. They are (1) all the families of the earth shall be blessed in Abraham, (2) that Abraham and Sarah should have a son, and (3) that in Isaac should Abraham's descendants be called. Paul has already alluded to the fruition of the promises in Galatians 3:8,14.

Paul next argued that seed was singular and not plural. The true seed of Abraham therefore is Christ. Now Paul's analogy may seem strange to us, for the word *seed* can be a collective noun in the

Hebrew and Greek just as it can be in English. However, in Genesis 12:12 a distinction is made between Ishmael and Isaac as far as inheritance is concerned. Paul was quoting from the text of the Greek Old Testament rather than the Hebrew and the word *seed* is singular there. In that sense then Paul made a distinction between Christ and the nation Israel in God's promise to Abraham. He seems to be saying that Christ is the true embodiment of what Israel was to be. Therefore, it is in him rather than in the national hope that God's promises to Abraham were to be realized. Just as Isaac replaced Ishmael in Abraham's inheritance, so Christ and his people have superseded national Israel as the recipients of God's promises to Abraham.

In verse 17 Paul shifted his argument back to the idea of the covenant which he introduced in verse 15. His major thrust is that, though the law intervened between the giving of the promise and the coming of Christ in fulfillment of the promise, it in no way annulled the promise. Paul was not arguing that the law was an intrusion into God's plans. Whatever the Judaizers may have said to the people of Galatia, Paul wanted his readers to know that the law could not supersede the promise which God made to Abraham and which had been fulfilled in Jesus Christ.

In verse 18 Paul continued his argument. The inheritance which God granted to Abraham and his descendants was based either on promise or on law. It couldn't be both. For Paul, law and promise were antitheses just as were law and faith. Undoubtedly the Judaizers had made much of the importance of keeping the ordinances of the law in order to enjoy the fullness of the promises which God had made to Abraham. Paul maintained that the law or the keeping of it had nothing to do with inheriting the promises which God made to Abraham. Hear his words: "But God granted it to Abraham by means of a promise." The word *it* as used by Paul has reference to the inheritance which Paul claimed for Christians as the spiritual heirs of God.

At this point a logical question was raised by Paul's argument. If God intended all the while to work out his purposes through Christ apart from the law, why did he give the law at all? Why didn't he just send Christ at the time he gave the law? Paul answered that the law was given because of flagrant and continual sin. This was God's way of dealing with transgressions until in the fullness of time he should send his Son as the seed of Abraham "to whom the promise had been made."

By his argument that Christ was the promised seed of Abraham, Paul maintained that the great promise of God to Abraham found in Genesis 12:3 found fruition. Among the things which God said to Abraham in that context is the promise that "in you all the families of the earth shall be blessed." Though the Jews did on occasion lower the barrier and allow Gentile prosyletes into partial covenant relationships, there was never a time in the history of the Jews when the promise of God to Abraham found fruition.

Primarily through the efforts of Paul the message of Christianity had been presented to the Gentiles of the Greco-Roman world of the first century. Christian congregations were springing up throughout the Mediterranean world because of Paul's missionary activities. However, a group of legalistic Jews were dogging Paul's footsteps teaching the Gentile converts that it was necessary for them to be circumcised and keep the law of Moses to enjoy fully the blessings of God in Christ.

Paul's letter to the Galatians is his answer to these critics of the true gospel. In response to their nefarious activities, Paul, under the leadership of God's Spirit, set forth this beautiful analogy concerning Christ as the true seed of Abraham. God's promise to Abraham had found fulfillment in Jesus Christ. Though the law had been a part of God's plan, it could not circumvent the actualization of God's promise to Abraham and its ultimate fruition in Jesus Christ.

15

The Coming Judge

But when the Son of man comes in his glory and all the angels with him, then shall he sit upon his glorious throne, And all of the nations shall be gathered before him, and he will separate them from one another as the shepherds separate the sheep from the goats, and he will set the sheep on his right hand and the goats on the left. Then shall the king say to those on his right hand, "Come you who are blessed of my Father, begin to inherit the kingdom prepared for you from the foundation of the world. For I hungered and you gave me to eat, I thirsted and you gave me drink, I was a stranger and you took me in, naked and you clothed me, sick and you cared for me, in prison and you came to me." Then shall those on his right hand answer him saying, "Lord when did we see you hungry and feed you, or thirsty and give you drink? And when did we see you a stranger and take you in, or naked and clothe you? And when did we see you sick or in prison and come to you?" And the king will answer and say to them, "Amen, I say to you, inasmuch as you did it to one of these my brothers even the least ones, you did it to me."

Then will he also say to those on the left hand, "Depart from me you cursed ones into the eternal fire which has been prepared for the devil and his angels. For I hungered and you gave me nothing to eat, I thirsted and you gave me no drink, I was a stranger and you did not take me in, naked and you did not clothe me, sick and in prison and you did not care for me." Then shall they answer saying, "Lord, when did we see you hungry or thirsty or a stranger or naked or sick or in prison and did not minister to you?" Then shall he answer them

saying, "Amen, I say to you in as much as you did not do it to one of
these least ones, you did it not to me." Then shall these depart into
eternal punishment, but the righteous to eternal life (Matt. 25:31-41).

God As Judge

In the Old Testament God is often pictured as judge. In Genesis
18:25 he is called the judge of all the earth. In Psalm 94:2 he is called
the judge of the earth who will bring judgment upon the proud. Isaiah
spoke of God as judge in 33:22. In the Old Testament God's role as
judge was based upon the fact that he was the giver of life and the
one who was able to take life. In 2 Kings 5 there is recorded the
episode of Naaman the Syrian general who was a leper. He was
encouraged to go to Israel to seek a cure from the prophet Elisha. He
went first to the king of Israel asking that he cure him. The king was
upset and replied: "Am I God, to kill and to make alive, that this man
is sending *word* to me to cure a man of his leprosy?" (v. 7, NASB). As
far as he was concerned, God had cursed him with leprosy, and God
would have to cure him of his disease.

The picture of God as the final arbiter in the affairs of men
pervades the Old Testament. God will vindicate the righteous and
bring the wicked to judgment. He is not only the one who judges
individuals, but he is the judge of nations. He brings his own people
Israel under judgment when they sin, but he also sits in judgment
upon the nations of the world. This is a recurring theme in the Psalms
and in the Prophets.

God is also recognized as judge in the New Testament. In Hebrews
12:23 he is spoken of as the Judge of all. In 1 Peter 1:17 he is
referred to as the "One who without respect to persons judges each
one according to his work." James 4:12 calls him the one Lawgiver
and judge, because he is the one who is able to save and to destroy.
There can be little doubt that God's activity as judge has been carried
over from the Old Testament by the writers of the New Testament.
This fact is borne out in almost every New Testament document.

Jesus As Judge

In New Testament thought there is also an integral connection between Jesus and judgment. The writers of the New Testament never express the idea that there is any sort of contradiction between the idea that God is judge and that judgment belongs to Jesus. Our Lord himself saw no contradiction here, but rather viewed himself as God's instrument in judgment. In John 5:30 he said: "I can do nothing by myself; as I hear I judge, and my judgment is right, because I do not seek my own will but the will of him who sent me." In Acts 10:42, in the midst of one of Peter's sermons, he said: "And he ordered us to preach to the people, and to testify solemnly that this is the One appointed by God to judge the living and the dead." The One of whom he spoke is, of course, Jesus.

In 2 Timothy 4:8 Paul referred to Jesus as "the righteous judge," so there is a sense in which the New Testament knows our Lord as judge in his own right. Paul had this in mind, when in 2 Corinthians 5:10 he said, "For it is necessary for all of us to appear before the judgment seat of Christ." Though Jesus is not often referred to by the title judge in the New Testament, his activity is surely described as that of judgment in many passages. In John 9:39 Jesus said: "For judgment I came into this world." Some may see a contradiction in this statement and the one in John 3:17 where it says: "For God did not send the Son into the world to judge the world," as well as Jesus' statement in John 12:37-38: "And if anyone hears my words and does not keep them, I do not judge him, for I came not to judge the world but to save the world. The one who rejects me and does not receive my words has one who judges him. The word which I spoke will judge him in the last day."

Jesus did not contradict himself. His primary task was to save the world, but for those who came into contact with him and rejected him, his life and teachings were a judgment upon them. The same is true today. Outside of the Gospels the concept of Jesus as judge is found in practically every section. Luke recorded the idea in Acts. When Paul preached to the Athenians as recorded in Acts 17, he spoke of Christ as the one through whom God will judge the world (v. 31). In the writings of Paul this idea is found several times. In Romans 2:16 he spoke of the day when "God will judge the secrets of men through Jesus Christ." In 1 Corinthians 4:4 he said that the Lord is the one who judges him. The word here is sometimes translated examine, and in this context it has to do with present judgment rather than final judgment.

Perhaps the most inclusive statement made by Paul in this regard is found in 2 Corinthians 5:10 where he said that we all must appear before the judgment seat of Christ. This has to do with final judgment, and it is all inclusive. Though the reference may be to God, there is a possible reference to Jesus as judge in 1 Peter 4:5 where he said that all must give an account before the one who is ready to judge the living and the dead. From the evidence presented, several conclusions can be drawn concerning Jesus as judge in the New Testament. (1) He is God's instrument in judgment, and (2) he judges in his own right. (3) His judgment is present, and (4) it is future. (5) His judgment is all inclusive.

I have purposely not treated the Synoptic Gospels (Matthew, Mark, and Luke) until now because the thrust there is somewhat different than it is in John, Acts, and the Epistles. In the first three Gospels Jesus is never referred to as judge, but his activity as judge is pervasive, particularly in certain of the parables as well as in the scene of the last judgment depicted in Matthew 25:31-46.

In the parable of the wheat and tares found in Matthew 13:24-30 the judgment motif is especially prominent and Jesus is prominent as the one who accomplishes the judgment (vv. 36-43). The judgment depicted here is a delayed judgment. Though the tares were recognized, they were allowed to grow until harvest. This is a picture of the future final judgment. The judgment depicted here is also a thoroughgoing one.

The parable of the drag net (Matt. 13:47-51) has the same thrust as the parable of the wheat and tares. Judgment is future, but it is thorough and final.

In Matthew 22:1-14 we find the foreboding parable of the king's wedding feast. The thrust of the parable is that judgment is certain when one rejects the king's invitation or even when one attempts to accept the king's invitation without coming on the king's terms. Those who rejected the king's invitation found that, when a king issued an invitation, it was not to be taken lightly. It could be rejected but not without consequences: The man who came to the feast without a wedding garment found that a king's invitation cannot be misconstrued without facing the consequences. The foreboding message of the parable is that man may say no to our Lord's invitation, but by doing so he does not write off the matter. Rather he only changes the circumstances under which he must face his judgment.

Perhaps the most vivid portrayal of Jesus as judge in the entire New Testament is found in Matthew 25:31-46. In this passage there is little doubt that Jesus claimed for himself the role of judge in that final day, even though he changed from the title Son of man to that of king in speaking of the role of judge. There are two things which should be stressed in this passage which warns of judgment to come. The first things are the basis used to determine the judgment. That basis has to do with relationships. Basically there are two relationships with which a person should be concerned. There is that vertical relationship which has to do with man and God. Then there is the horizontal relationship which has to do with man and man. All too often we seek to divorce our vertical relationship from our horizontal relationship, but according to this passage, this approach to life simply is untenable. You will notice that the primary emphasis in the passage is upon the vertical relationship. The king emphasized that those being judged had seen him in need and had responded appropriately or had not responded. The ultimate criterion in determining this vertical relationship, however, has to do with the horizontal. To the extent that you responded to the needs of the little people around you, just to that extent have you responded to my needs is the essence of the king's reply to those before the judgment throne.

The second thing that should be noted in this passage is the surprise or shock of both groups. The sheep reply: "When did we see you in need and not respond?" "When you responded or failed to respond to the needs of the little people around you!" is the reply of the king. The emphasis may strike us as strange, but remember these are the words of our Lord.

The thrust of the judgment scene is that, when our vertical relationship is correct, it will be reflected in our horizontal relationship. If we love God, we will show it in service to our fellowman.

16
The Great I Am

The Jews answered and said to him, "Did we not say correctly that you are a Samaritan and have a demon?" Jesus answered, "I do not have a demon, but I honor my Father, and you dishonor me. Now I do not seek my own glory, there is One who is seeking and judging. Amen amen I say to you, if anyone keeps my word, he shall never see death." The Jews said: "Now we know that you have a demon. Abraham died as did the prophets, and you say, if anyone keeps my word they shall not taste death. You are not greater than our Father Abraham, who died, are you? The prophets died also, who do you make yourself to be?" Jesus answered: "If I glorify myself, my glory is nothing. My Father is the One glorifying me, whom you say he is our God. And you have not known him, but I know him. Even if I should say that I do not know him, I shall be like you a liar, but I do know him and keep his word. Abraham our father rejoiced to see my day, and he saw it and was glad." The Jews therefore said to him: "You are not yet fifty years old and have seen Abraham." Jesus said to them: "Amen amen I say to you, before Abraham came to be I am." They therefore took up stones to throw at him, but Jesus hid himself and went out of the temple (John 8:48-59).

Recorded in Exodus 3 is the account of Moses' encounter with God at the bush which burned but was not consumed. In that encounter God identified himself as the God of Abraham, Isaac, and Jacob and instructed Moses to go to the aid of the people of God in Egypt. Moses asked God to reveal his name so that he would know what to tell the people of Israel concerning him. God replied to Moses: "I am the THE BEING." This is the translation from the Septuagint (the Greek Old Testament). The form used here indicates that God was emphasizing his eternal existence. God has no beginning and no end; he is the Eternal One. Others have argued that the form here in the Hebrew does not so much emphasize the eternal existence of God as it does his action and presence in the affairs of men. Still others have suggested that there is here a strong indication of God's faithfulness to his people through his positive intervention in the affairs of history. This well may be true, but the fact remains that the emphasis of Jesus' statement in John 8:58 is on his eternal existence. There surely is no positive proof that Jesus had the statement of God in Exodus 3:14 in mind when he made his assertion recorded in John 8:58. However, the similarity of the two statements in the Greek text of John and the Greek text of Exodus surely leads on to postulate at least the possibility of the connection between the two.

In the great Christological passages found In 1 John 1:1-4; Philippians 2:5-11; Colossians 1:15-20; and Hebrews 1:1-3 the preexistent glory of Christ is expressed in terms that indicate the perpetuity of his being. However, only in the Gospel according to John do we find this idea on the lips of Jesus. There are several instances recorded in John where Jesus expressed the importance of his being and his work by the use of the phrase "I am." This phrase as it appears in the Greek text is emphatic in its expression.

To the crowd in the Temple (John 8:12) and to his disciples prior to healing the man blind from birth (9:5), Jesus said, "I am the light of the world." The day after he had fed the multitudes they sought him out again thinking that he would care for their physical needs once more. Jesus urged them to be more concerned for their spiritual needs than for their physical needs. They challenged him to demonstrate his greatness by feeding them as Moses had fed their fathers in the wilderness with mana. In John 6:35 Jesus made the statement: "I am the bread of life." Because of who he is, he can give the true sustenance of life. In the shepherd discourse of John 10 Jesus used this phrase more than once. He said: "I am the door of the sheep" (v. 7). He also said: "I am the good shepherd" (v. 11). Prior to the raising of Lazarus, Jesus was speaking with Martha who was remonstrating with him because he had not come earlier. "Your brother will rise again," said Jesus. Martha said to him: "I know that he shall be raised in the resurrection in the last day." Then in John 11:25 Jesus made this marvelous statement: "I am the resurrection and the life, the one who believes in me shall never die." Then in John 15 Jesus gave the beautiful analogy of the vine and the branches. In verse 1 he said: "I am the vine."

The greatest "I am" statement of Jesus, however, is found in John 8:58 where he said: "Before Abraham came to be, I am." This statement was made in a context of conflict with the Jewish leaders. Jesus had previously stated that the Jews were not legitimate children of Abraham but were children of the devil and were in league with the devil in their opposition to him. In John 8:48 they turned on Jesus with all of their fury and accused him of being a demon-possessed Samaritan. Jesus replied that he was only honoring his Father, but that they were dishonoring Jesus by their words and actions. Jesus tried once again to appeal to them through the eternal nature of his message, but this just infuriated them more and convinced them that he was demented.

At the climax of this verbal exchange, Jesus told them that Abraham rejoiced to see his day. They wanted to know how he, a man who was less than fifty years old could have seen Abraham. To this statement he made this claim: "Before Abraham came to be, I am." Those who heard him were so incensed that they took up stones to throw at him. They understood what Jesus meant by the statement, and they considered it to be the audacious and exaggerated claim of one whose earthly origin they knew. In their eyes he was only a man and a relatively young one at that.

If Jesus had said to them, "I was before Abraham," he would have been expressing a simple priority of being. However, by the use of the phrase "I am" he was emphasizing a timeless existence. The verb that he used of Abraham is the verb for becoming, and it indicated that there was a point at which Abraham came into being. Thus there is a contrast here between the created and the uncreated or the temporal and the eternal. His claim undoubtedly is that he was making himself equal to God. Whether or not he had in his mind the declaration of God to Moses in Exodus 3:14 cannot be ascertained. As I stated earlier, however, there is a strong probability that he did.

Three things are implied by Jesus' use of this form of address to the Jewish leaders. They are: (1) revelation, (2) deity, and (3) judgment. Though the Jewish leaders did not accept either of these ideas, they definitely are present in the context. Throughout the episodes recorded in chapters 7—8 of the Gospel of John, is the recurring theme of revelation. Jesus had sought to make himself known to the people by his appearance at the Feast of Tabernacles and by his pronouncement that he could supply living water to all who would come to him and believe in him. Then he used the analogy that he was the Light of the world and that whoever should follow him would not go on walking in darkness. The clearer his claims became the more recalcitrant became the Jewish leaders. The climax in the process of Jesus' revelation of himself came at the height of their rebellion against his teaching. There can be no doubt that couched within this assertion in John 8:58 there is a strong note of revelation concerning the personal claim of Jesus for himself.

That Jesus claimed for himself deity by this statement cannot be denied logically. The words which he used and the grammatical construction, as well as the reaction of the Jewish leaders, all point to a claim of deity. On the lips of another these words would have constituted blasphemy. This is why the Jewish leaders sought to stone him. They refused to be influenced by his teaching or by his works, and they therefore considered his claim to be blasphemous.

Basically Jesus was claiming for himself perpetual and eternal existence independent of the realm of time by his assertion. In contrast to himself Abraham came into existence at a specific point in time. He, on the other hand, has no beginning nor end, and his being is totally independent of time. Had he not been divine, his claim would have been an audacious one to be sure.

Perhaps the least obvious implication of his statement is that of judgment. Had he not left the Temple, the rulers surely would have caused bodily injury to him. Apparently they had the upper hand and were trying to bring their wrath down upon him. However, underneath the currents of their angry response to Jesus' claim is the judgment which his claim had already made upon them. The fact that they responded negatively to the claim does not make the judgment any less real. Everyone must stand before the claims of Jesus and respond to them. Our response to his claims determines the course of divine judgment in our lives.

Jesus' answer to the Jews in John 8:58 is just one of several places in the New Testament where the eternality of his being is indicated. This one, however, is significant for it is the only instance where we find a saying on the lips of Jesus that clearly indicates his own assessment of himself in this light. As the "Great I Am," he reveals himself as deity and brings us under his judgment.

17

A Prophet Like Moses

The Lord your God will raise up for you a prophet like me from among you, from your countrymen, you shall listen to him (Deut. 18:15, NASB).

And the Lord said to me, They have spoken well. I will raise up a prophet among their countrymen like you, and I will put my words in his mouth, and he shall speak to them all that I command him (Deut. 18:17-18, NASB).

And this is the testimony of John, when the Jews from Jerusalem sent to him priests and Levites in order that they might ask him: "Who are you?" And he confessed and did not deny, and he confessed: "I am not the Messiah." And they asked him: "Who then? Are you Elijah?" And he said: "I am not." "Are you that prophet?" And he answered: "No" (John 1:19-21).

And Jesus came and his disciples with him into the region of Caesarea Philippi, and in the way he asked his disciples saying to them, "Who do men say that I am?" And they answered him saying: "John the Baptist, and others Elijah, and others that you are one of the prophets" (Mark 8:27-28).

Moses said: "A prophet shall the Lord your God raise up for you from among your brethren like me" (Acts 3:22).

Though the title "prophet" is not one of the more popular titles for Jesus among Christians today, it was surely one of the more popular titles for Jesus while he was on earth. It probably was not used of him in a messianic sense until after the resurrection, but the title was used of him; and he used it of himself during his ministry. The Jews looked for a series of prophets to appear just prior to the coming of Messiah, and they looked for Messiah to come in the prophetic tradition. This is clear from their interrogation of John the Baptist recorded in John 1:19-21. What is not clear from their questions is what they meant by the term "that prophet." Some have suggested that Jeremiah was meant. Possibly they had reference to that prophet like Moses spoken of in Deuteronomy 18:18, but this is by no means certain. There is little evidence that prophet was a messianic designation among the Jews.

There is ample evidence from the Gospels that the Jews of Jesus' time took him to be a prophet. When Jesus asked the disciples what the people were saying about him (Mark 8:27), their answer reflected a prophetic interpretation of Jesus' work. That the disciples' answer was an accurate reflection of popular opinion about Jesus is generally accepted. The question has been raised as to why Jesus asked them this question at all. The suggestion has been made that, while Jesus had been involved in ministry to individuals, he had not been in a position to hear what the crowds had been saying about him. On the other hand, the disciples had been circulating among the crowds and would have had ample opportunity to hear what the people were saying about Jesus. It is interesting to note that the common people had not as yet thought of Jesus as the Messiah. They were, however, convinced that he was a great prophet.

That Jesus considered himself a prophet can be seen in several places in the Gospels. After his disappointing and unsuccessful visit to Nazareth (Mark 6:1-6), he said: "A prophet is not without honor except in his own country, among his own kin and among his own household." When he was warned of the danger that awaited him in Jerusalem, he replied: "Nevertheless I must journey on today and tomorrow and the next, for it cannot be that a prophet should perish outside of Jerusalem." Though these references surely do not indicate that Jesus thought of his work exclusively as that of a prophet, they surely are indicative of the fact that he viewed his work as prophetic.

The earliest Christians regarded Jesus' prophetic work as an important part of his task. After Jesus' resurrection, he appeared to two who were on their way to Emmaus. As they conversed with Jesus, one of the two named Cleopas said to Jesus: "The things about Jesus the Nazarene, who was a prophet mighty in deed and word in the sight of God and all the people" (Luke 24:19, NASB). As Peter preached in the Temple area after the Pentecost experience, he referred to Jesus as the prophet like Moses (Acts 3:22). Though this theme was never developed as one of the chief Christological themes of the early church, it surely was one of the earliest of the Christological themes to receive attention by the teachers among the earliest Christians.

There are several incidents in the life of Jesus which parallel incidents in the life of Moses. These are seen most clearly in the Gospel of Matthew, and this has led some scholars to conclude that Matthew was presenting Jesus as a second Moses. That these parallels can be seen is true, but it cannot be proven objectively that this was Matthew's purpose in recording these parallels.

In the case of Moses, as in the case of Jesus, hostile kings ordered the slaughter of all male children. The Pharaoh was disturbed over the rapid growth in population among the Hebrews, so he ordered all male infants slain. Moses was hidden in the river and was found by the daughter of Pharaoh; thus he was delivered. Out of fear and jealousy, because he thought a rival king had been born, Herod the Great ordered all male infants in the village of Nazareth under the age of two to be slain. Because of divine intervention through a dream, Joseph took Mary and the infant Jesus into Egypt. Thus our Lord was spared the wrath of Herod.

When Moses was a grown man, he had to flee once again from the wrath of the Pharaoh because he killed an Egyptian. He fled to Midian where he sojourned for forty years. Jesus' sojourn in Egypt as a child may be seen as a parallel to the sojourn of Moses in Midian.

When Jesus was in the desert prior to his temptation experience, he fasted for forty days. When Moses went up on the Mount to receive the law, he was gone for forty days, and during this time he fasted.

Moses went up into the Mount to receive the law which he later delivered to the people. Jesus went up on a mountain, and when the people came to him, he delivered what is commonly referred to as the Sermon on the Mount. Some have even tried to see in the Sermon on the Mount a new law for those who are in the kingdom of heaven. This probably is carrying the parallel too far, for Jesus militated against legalism rather than placing his sanction upon it.

Though there probably is not a parallel to be seen here, it is interesting to note that, when Jesus was transfigured on the mountain, Moses was present along with Elijah. Undoubtedly Moses is representative of the law as Elijah is of the prophets. Their presence illustrates the Old Testament's relationship to Jesus and Jesus' relationship to the Old Testament. As the Old Testament prophesied the coming of Jesus, so Jesus fulfills the Old Testament. Thus the transfiguration of Jesus illustrates in bold relief the unbroken revelation of God.

These parallels in the experiences of Jesus and Moses are interesting and are instructive for study. However, I think it should be emphasized that Matthew was not presenting Jesus as one in a series with Moses, Elijah, and Jeremiah. He presented Jesus not just as another great prophet or lawgiver but as Emmanuel—God with us (Matt. 1:23).

Probably the reason the early theologians of Christianity did not develop the concept of Jesus as prophet is that which has been stated above. There is by the very nature of the title the danger that Jesus would be seen as one in a series of great men rather than as the unique Son of God.

18

Victor

Now when this corruptible shall be clothed with incorruption and this mortal shall be clothed with immortality, then shall come to pass the word which has been written: "Death is swallowed up in victory, Oh death, where is your victory? Oh death, where is your sting? Now the sting of death is sin, and the power of sin is the law; but thanks be to God who has given us the victory through our Lord Jesus Christ (1 Cor. 15:54-57).

Having disarmed the rules and authorities, he made a public display of them triumphing over them in it (Col. 2:15).

But to each one of us was this grace given according to the measure of the gift of Christ. Wherefore it says: "When he ascended on high he led a host of captives captive, and he gave gifts to men." (Now, he ascended, what is it except that he descended into the lower parts of the earth? The one who descended is himself the one who ascended high above all the heavens, in order that he might fill up all things.) And he gave to some apostles, and some prophets, and some evangelists, and some pastors and teachers, for the equipping of the saints for the work of ministering, for the building up of the body of Christ, until we all attain to the unity of the faith even the full knowledge of the Son of God, unto a mature man, unto the measure of the stature of the fulness of Christ (Eph. 4:7-13).

The kingdom of the world has become the kingdom of our Lord and of his Christ, and he shall reign forever and ever (Rev. 11:15b).

The truth that Christ is victor is a vital theme throughout the New

Testament, but this idea is expressed perhaps most eloquently in the epistles of Paul. There are two realms in which the New Testament properly speaks of Christ as victor. They are (1) the past and (2) the future. There is a sense in which Christ has achieved victory, and because of this, the believer can share in his victory. There is another sense in which his final victory is yet to be, and the believer will also share in that victory. Both are quite real and give legitimate cause for rejoicing.

As Victor He Conquered Death

Death strikes fear into the heart of the bravest. So dreaded is death that the word is almost taboo in our culture today. Rather than speak plainly of death we have developed euphemisms and circumlocutions to avoid the mention of it. When speaking of a person's death, we say "they passed on" or "they went to their reward," or in some like way we avoid the mention of the unpleasant subject of death. Often, when a person is dying and all parties involved are aware of the fact, the subject is still carefully avoided, to the detriment of all involved.

For the Christian this need not be for Christ has conquered death. By his resurrection he tells us that death is not the end. Rather it is a bridge over which we pass from the realm of time into that of eternity. We can shout with Paul in 1 Corinthians 15:57: "Thanks be to God who gives us the victory through our Lord Jesus Christ." This is our theology in theory, and we should make it our theology in practice. Our Lord has conquered death, and because of this, we need have no fear of death. Truly he is victor.

As Victor He Vanquished the Powers

Death by crucifixion was the ultimate insult in the Roman world of the first century of the Christian era. This means of execution was reserved for slaves and the most despised classes of criminals. The stigma of the cross can scarcely be appreciated by us today who view it as the beautiful means of God's redemption of mankind. Paul spoke of the cross as foolishness to the Greeks and a stumbling block for the Jews. The scandal of a crucified Messiah had to be overcome as the gospel confronted a pagan world.

Paul saw the cross as the scene of a cosmic conflict between God in Christ and the evil powers of this age. Christ confronted the age powers on the cross, and he triumphed over them. Paul did not identify these age powers other than by various titles such as rulers and authorities (Col. 2:15). I doubt that we should seek to do more than to say that whatever or whoever they are they surely are evil and are aligned with Satan.

As victor at the cross, Christ disarmed the powers and made a public display of them. The word for disarmed literally was used to describe the act of removing one's wearing apparel. Here the word was used in a figurative sense of stripping the powers of their weapons in this cosmic conflict. Evil appeared to triumph that day as life ebbed from the Son of God, but in reality the cross represents the triumph of God in Christ over the forces of evil. The word for public display has to do with a public exhibition of the vanquished in a triumphal procession. Our Lord not only stripped these cosmic powers of their weaponry, but also he made a public exhibit of them in a triumphal procession.

As Victor He Gives Gifts to His People

This triumphal procession in which Christ exhibited the vanquished powers is described by Paul in Ephesians 4:7-13. Paul's vivid description of this heavenly triumphal procession in Ephesians 4:8 is a quotation from Psalm 68:18. His explanation of it in the following verses indicates that it took place in heaven. The triumphant Christ paraded the vanquished age powers before the hosts of heaven and bestowed gifts upon his people.

The Roman triumvum of which this is a replica came at the conclusion of successful battles, and it always took place in the city of

Rome. The triumphant general brought his prisoners of war along with the booty seized in war to the city of Rome. There with his triumphant soldiers he led his host of captives through the streets of the city of Rome in a festive parade. During this parade, he bestowed gifts upon the populace from the booty seized in the conflict.

Our Lord's triumph did not take place in an earthly city, for his battle was a spiritual one of cosmic proportions. Having vanquished these age powers on the cross, he led them captive in a triumphal march through the heavenly city. From that vantage point, he has bestowed gifts of his spiritual conquest upon his people.

Paul enumerated these gifts in the form of functional offices within the church in the Ephesian passage. They are: (1) apostles, (2) prophets, (3) evangelists, (4) pastors, and (5) teachers. All of these gifts have a single purpose. They are to be used in equipping the saints for the work of service.

Because Christ was victorious, Christians also will be victorious. The victory has been won in this cosmic conflict in the sphere of eternity, though it has yet to be fully realized in the plane of history. The church cannot fail; the purposes of God will not allow it to fail. The church may falter and be the victim of fragmentation, but ultimately the purposes of God will prevail. In the words of the hymn writer Samuel J. Stone: "The church's one foundation is Jesus Christ her Lord."

On that final day when the kingdoms of this world shall become the kingdom of our Lord, the redeemed church will stand victorious in the victory of her reigning Lord, and shout with the hosts of heaven: "He is worthy who has overcome!"